# Landscapes of
# MENORCA

## a countryside guide
### *Second edition*

**Rodney Ansell**

SUNFLOWER
BOOKS

*Dedicated to Helen*

**Second edition 1996; reprint
with Stop Press 1997**
Sunflower Books
12 Kendrick Mews
London SW7 3HG, UK

ISBN 1-85691-081-4

# *Important note to the reader* ____

We have tried to ensure that the descriptions and maps in this book are error-free at press date. The book will be updated, where necessary, whenever future printings permit. It will be very helpful for us to receive your comments (sent in care of the publishers, please) for the updating of future printings.

We also rely on those who use this book — especially walkers — to take along a good supply of common sense when they explore. Conditions change fairly rapidly on Menorca, and *storm damage or bulldozing may make a route unsafe at any time.* If the route is not as we outline it here, and your way ahead is not secure, return to the point of departure. *Never attempt to complete a tour or walk under hazardous conditions!* Please read carefully the country code on page 10, the walking notes on pages 30 and 31, and the introductory comments at the beginning of each tour and walk (regarding road conditions, equipment, grade, distances and time, etc). Explore *safely,* while at the same time respecting the beauty of the countryside.

*Cover photograph: Golden Farm*
*Title page: Taula at Talatí de Dalt*

Photographs by the author (pages 26, 43, 44, 54-5, 59, 62, 68, 89, 91, 95, 99, 107, 111, 128); Helen Ansell (pages 4, 76); Hans Losse (pages 1, 2, 3, 15, 20-1, 23, 25, 28-9, 39, 42, 47, 56, 60-1, 65, 70, 78-9, 83, 84, 93, 100, 122, 134); Alan Goodin (page 71)
Maps by John Theasby and Pat Underwood, based on Spanish military maps (with kind permission of the Servicio Geográfico del Ejército)
Drawings by John Theasby
A CIP catalogue record for this book is available from the British Library.
Printed and bound in Great Britain by KPC Group, Ashford, Kent

10 9 8 7 6 5 4 3

# ❀ Contents _____

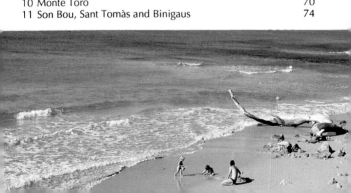

## 4 Landscapes of Menorca

Menorca's
fields are
a riot of
wild
flowers in
spring.
This
photo-
graph was
taken on
Walk 11,
near Son
Benet.

# ❀ Preface

Menorca is the island people fall in love with … the one they go back to year after year, the island where they go to retire. And no wonder. For in addition to all the normal attractions you expect from a holiday island — lively resorts, good safe beaches, day-long sunshine, splendid restaurants — Menorca has something special. Such as dozens of lovely untouched beaches and a gorgeous countryside. And, as if that were not enough, it has the densest concentration of prehistoric monuments in Europe.

Although only small, much of the island is isolated and, without the help this book provides, difficult for the visitor to penetrate. Two days' motoring will enable you to see most of that part of the island which is accessible by car (by no means all of it). As for the rest, it is gentle walking country and the remoter regions are best explored on foot — or by bicycle.

## Acknowledgements

My thanks to the following people, who have helped me with the preparation of the material for this book:

Señora María Angeles Hernandez Gómez, Cronista Arxivera Municipal of Mahón, and her colleagues in the Ajuntament, for advice on rights of way (and suggesting Walk 2); Señor Lorenzo Cavallir of the Department of Works of the Consell Insular; Sr Rafael Valls, Legal Attaché at the Spanish Embassy in London, for his advice on Spanish law; Alan Goodin, for his help with the island's flora and birds; Frankie and John Cross, who not only drew on many years' familiarity with (and love of) Menorca to advise me, but also found out and brought back all those things I had overlooked. Very special thanks to my wife, Helen, for her constant encouragement and readiness to act as guinea-pig, and to my publishers. Finally, to the many people who have written to me with information and suggestions, several of which are included in this edition.

## Useful books

Your library or local bookshop can suggest the best general guides, prior to your departure. When you are on the island, you should be able to find the following useful reference books: Antoni Bonner, *Plantes de les Balears;* Hoskin and Waldren, *Taulas and Talayots;* Rev Fernando Marti, *History of Menorca.*

If you enjoy using this book, and you would like to explore the countryside on the other Balearic Islands, Sunflower also publishes *Landscapes of Mallorca* and *Landscapes of Ibiza and Formentera.* Both are available from your local library or bookshop.

#  Introduction

**H**ow to get there

Menorca is easily reached by air to Mahón airport. From May to October package holidays and 'flight only' arrangements from various airports throughout the UK are plentiful. Monarch Airlines operates a scheduled service to the island from London's Luton Airport: there are two flights a week in summer and one a week from November to April.

**G**eography

The island is small — only some 50 kilometres (30 miles) by 20 kilometres (12 miles) at its widest point. It is also a fairly flat island. There are low hills in the north, but there are no mountains. At 358m (1175ft), Monte Toro, in the centre of the island, is the highest point. This makes for easy walking.

The most significant geographical feature is the *cala*, the creek or fjord terminating in a tiny sandy beach. These lie at the end of the ravines, or *barrancos*, which cut through the southern half of the island particularly. Because of the many *barrancos,* the basic road pattern of Menorca is a central highway (the C721), from which arms branch off to the various beach resorts *(urbanizaciones)*. There is no coastal road running round the island. Indeed, both circular drives and circular walks are difficult to plan.

The vast majority of the population lives in five towns (Mahón, Alaior, Es Mercadal, Ferreries, and Ciutadella) strung across the centre of the island along the C721. Holidaymakers generally stay in a number of resorts dotted around the coast, mostly in the south and west. The rest of the island is given over to isolated farms, which connect with the road system and each other by rough tracks and newly-surfaced lanes — the setting for most of the walks suggested in this book. The fields, mostly used for dairy cattle, are separated by dry-stone walls, and sometimes, if you do any of the walks, you will be called upon to scale them. In some cases, protruding stones *(botadores)* help you over these hurdles. (It is not difficult to climb over the walls on any of the walks I have described.)

6

# Weather

July and August are hot and sunny. While there will be the occasional overcast or windy day, these will be infrequent. During spring, early summer and autumn, expect more cloudy days and rain. Menorca is the wettest of the Balearic Islands. It is the price paid for its gorgeous vegetation and abundant bird life. But it will not be cold, and there will be many hot and sunny days as well. A feature of the winter months is a strong, sometimes quite cold wind which at times blows from the north.

If you go to Menorca hoping to do some walking, the overcast days are a bonus — it is far more enjoyable walking then than in full sunshine. Again, provided you have adequate protective clothing, the walks described here are an excellent alternative to paperback novels or gin rummy as a way of dealing with those cloudy days.

# Where to stay

The bulk of the holiday accommodation is to be found in the beach resorts. There are some hotels, but many people stay in holiday villas. There is a shortage of domestic help: the population is small and fully employed. You will look in vain for signs of poverty. Hardly any accommodation is available between November and April. The exceptions would be the Hotel Alfonso III in Ciutadella and some small *hostales* in Mahón. At Easter things begin to stir, and in May the hotels begin their season.

# Getting about on the island

A fairly frequent **bus service** plies between Mahón and Ciutadella along the C721, calling at the three intervening towns where there are bus stops (*paradas fijas*) whose locations change regularly. The bus leaves Mahón from Avinguda J M Quadrado, near the Plaça de S'Esplanada, and Ciutadella from Carrer Barcelona, off the Camí de Maó. A less frequent service goes from Mahón to Fornells via Arenal and Son Parc. The services to the beach resorts only operate in the summer, running at staggered intervals. Some begin in April, others in May, and yet others in June. These link the southern resorts with Mahón, and the northwestern ones with Ciutadella. Bus timetables are shown on pages 131-132. Don't rely solely on these, however. As soon as you arrive on the island, update these timetables by getting 'first-hand' information from the bus stations mentioned above, the tourist offices, or the bus stops. Buses generally run to time but, to be on the safe side, always arrive about ten minutes early. (Most of the walks described in this book can be reached by bus. Not all walks will be convenient from your resort, but there will be some that are. A few walks can only be reached by car.)

**Taxis** are only a phone call away, should you miss your bus. The tourist office in Mahón can provide you with a list of firms and telephone numbers. Hotel reception will always be ready to give assistance. All fares should be ascertained in advance.

The package tour couriers arrange **coach tours** which get you to all the tourist points of interest, but never off the beaten track. **Boat trips** around the coast are also arranged by the tour companies, or can be booked privately from Mahón, Es Castell and Ciutadella harbours. These often provide a barbecue lunch at a beach.

**Bicycles** can be readily hired, and the countryside south of Ciutadella in particular lends itself to exploration in this way. But be warned: the tarmac roads have a habit of turning into rough tracks — although these are ideal for mountain bikes!

## Language hints

In the tourist centres you hardly need know any Spanish. But out in the countryside, a few words of the language will be helpful, especially if you lose your way. Here's an — almost — foolproof way to communicate in Spanish. First, memorise the few short key questions and their possible answers, given below.

Then, when you have your 'mini-speech' memorised, *always ask the many questions you can concoct from it in such a way that you get a 'sí' (yes) or 'no' answer.* Never ask an open-ended question such as 'Where is the main road?' Instead, ask the question and then suggest the most likely answer yourself. For instance: 'Good day, sir. Please — where is the path to Ferreries? Is it straight ahead?' Now, unless you get a 'sí' response, try: 'Is it to the left?'

If you go through the list of answers to your own question, you will eventually get a 'sí' response, and this is more reassuring than relying on sign language.

Following are the most likely situations in which you may have to practise your Spanish. The dots (...) show where you will fill in the name of your destination. Ask a local person — perhaps someone at your hotel — to help you with the pronunciation of place names.

## ▪ Asking the way
### Key questions

| English | Spanish | Pronunciation |
|---|---|---|
| Good day | Buenos días | Boo-**eh**-nohs **dee**-ahs |
| sir (madam, miss) | señor (señora, señorita) | sen-**yor** (sen-**yor**-ah, sen-yor-**ee**-tah) |
| Please — | Por favor — | Poor fah-**vor** — |
| where is | dónde está | **dohn**-day es-**tah** |
| the road to ... ? | la carretera a ... ? | lah cah-reh-**teh**-rah ah... ? |
| the footpath to ...? | la senda de ... ? | lah **sen**-dah day ... ? |
| the way to ... ? | el camino a ... ? | el cah-**mee**-noh ah ... ? |
| the bus stop? | la parada? | lah pah-**rah**-dah? |
| Many thanks. | Muchas gracias. | **Moo**-chas **gra**-thee-ahs. |

### Possible answers

| English | Spanish | Pronunciation |
|---|---|---|
| Is it here? | Está aquí? | es-**tah** ah- **kee**? |
| there? | allí? | ahl-**yee**? |
| straight ahead? | todo recto? | **toh**-doh **rayk**-toh? |
| behind? | detrás? | day-**tras**? |
| right? | a la derecha? | ah lah day-**ray**-chah? |
| left? | a la izquierda? | ah lah eeth-kee-**er**-dah? |
| above? | arriba? | ah-**ree**-bah? |
| below? | abajo? | ah-**bah**-hoh? |

## ▪ Asking a taxi driver to take you somewhere and return for you, or asking a taxi to meet you at a certain place and time

| English | Spanish | Pronunciation |
|---|---|---|
| Please — | Por favor — | Poor fah-**vor** — |
| take us to ... | llévanos a ... | l-**yay**-vah-nohs ah ... |
| and return | y venga buscarnos | ee **vain**-gah boos-**kar**-nohs |
| at (place) at (time) | a ... a ...* | ah (place) ah (time)* |

*Point out the time on your watch.

# P lace names
The majority of place names on Menorca are the names of farmhouses. Occasionally you will see the name written large across the façade of the house. Where a settlement of any kind has to be named, from talayotic village to *urbanización,* it invariably takes its name from the farm on whose land it originates.

Generally the names are old. Many go back to the days of the Moors and are in Arabic, but most are Menorquín, the old language of the island, derived from Catalan. Some are in modern Catalan, and a few in Spanish. A number of words occur again and again, and with the hope that it may add interest to your excursions, I offer (on page 10) an explanation of the most frequent.

Firstly, however, some pronunciation hints are called for. In Menorquín 'ç' is pronounced as 's', 'll' as 'y' and 'x' as 'sh'. Here again, I do urge you to get some tips on pronunciation from a local person.

*torre* — a tower (sometimes corrupted to *turru* or *torr*). Menorca is full of towers, from prehistoric *talayots* to the watchtowers of the 17th and 18th centuries, by way of the fortified farmhouses of the Middle Ages, and a great many names include this element.

*es, sa, ses* — these are Menorquín equivalents of the Spanish *el, la, los/las*. *En, na* are variants of *es* and *sa*, used when referring to people, including proper names. All the above mean the same thing: 'the', as does *els* (Catalan) and *al* (Arabic).

*san* (Spanish), *sant* (Catalan), and *santa* (common to both Spanish and Catalan) mean saint: thus Sant Joan = San Juán = Saint John; Sant Jaume = San Jaime = Saint James.

*cova* or *cove* — a cave
*cala* — a creek or cove
*barranco* — a gorge
*son* — a large farmhouse
*bou* — an ox
*lloc, lluc* — a Moorish word for a farmhouse
*bini* — a very common Moorish word meaning 'sons'
*nou* — new
*vell* (also *vella, vei, vey*) — old
*de dalt* — higher
*de baix* — lower
*de devant* — in front
*de derrera* — behind

The six above entries are usually found in pairs. As families grew, and the sons built their homes nearby, the new farms were distinguished in this way from the parents' farm.

In recent years there has been a strong revival of the Menorquín language. Many Spanish names of both towns and streets have been altered to Menorquín ones, and many of the signs indicating public buildings, etc have also been revised. Some of the most common Menorquín words, with Spanish and English equivalents, follow:

**Towns:**

Maó — Mahón
Alaior — Alayor
Es Migjorn (Gran) — San Cristobal
Sant Lluís — San Luís

Ciutadella — Ciudadela
Ferreries — Ferrerías
Sant Climent — San Clemente
Es Castell — Villa-Carlos

**Streets, etc:**

carrer (calle) — street
plaça (plaza) — square
ajuntament (ayuntamiento) — town hall
centre ciutat (centro ciudad) — city centre

costa (cuesta) — hill
avinguda (avenida) — avenue
mercat (mercado) — market
platja (playa) — beach
camí (camino) — road

**Shops:**

obert (abierto) — open

tancat (cerrado) — closed

**The name of the island:**

The Romans called it Minorica, from which the English name Minorca was derived. It means the 'smaller' island (Majorca being the larger one). The Spanish equivalents are Menorca and Mallorca.

# Country code

Experienced ramblers are used to following a country code; tourists perhaps less so. Please heed the following guidelines during your visit to Menorca.

- Do not light fires.
- Do not frighten animals.
- Walk quietly through all hamlets and villages.
- Leave all gates just as you find them. Although you may not see any animals, the gates *do* have a purpose — generally to keep cattle or sheep in (or out of) an area.
- Protect all wild and cultivated plants. Don't try to pick wild flowers or uproot saplings. Fruit and other crops are someone's private property and should not be touched.
- Never walk over cultivated land (unless there is an explicit instruction to do so in the text, as in Walk 14).
- Take all your litter away with you.
- Walkers — Do not take risks! Do not attempt walks beyond your capacity, and do not wander off the paths described here, especially if it is late in the day. **Do not walk alone**, and *always* tell a responsible person exactly where you are going and what time you plan to return. Remember, if you become lost or injure yourself, it may be a long time before you are found. On any but a very short walk close to towns or villages, take some extra food, water, and warm clothing. A torch and whistle, even a compass, might be carried as well. *Do* read the guidelines on grade and equipment for each walk you plan.

# Prehistoric monuments

Menorca is home to the greatest concentration of prehistoric monuments on earth. It is only recently that many of them have been excavated, restored, or cleared of the vegetation that for centuries had overwhelmed them. Very many more await excavation. Several of the walks in this book include visits to some of the most interesting of these monuments.

The people of ancient Menorca worked with stone. The island is lacking in commercially useful metal ores, and there are no large trees for timber. Stone on the other hand abounds: south of a line drawn roughly from Cala Morell to Mahón via Ferreries, a young and easily-worked limestone is found, which nevertheless becomes hard and durable when exposed to the atmosphere.

There are five principal kinds of building: caves, *talayots*, *taulas*, hypostyle chambers, and *navetas*.

## Caves *(illustrated on pages 17, 76 and 132)*

After 2500 BC the earliest inhabitants carved out caves for themselves to live in. Those who suppose that cavemen were primitive savages inhabiting natural holes in the cliffs will be totally unprepared for the sophisticated craftsmanship of these troglodytic homes, all of which were carefully and skilfully chiselled out of the rock. Later generations moved out of the caves between 1400 and 1000 BC, and for the next thousand years they were used only as burial chambers.

### Talayots (illustrated on pages 54-55, 59 and 60-61)
These great conical mounds of stones, 5-10m (15-30ft) high, are very common on the island. Many are solid; some have an inside chamber and passage. All of them are now truncated. It is not known what purpose they served. Many suggestions have been made. Perhaps they had a timber house on top — for the local chieftain. Or they could have been defence towers, farmhouses, or storerooms. They are always associated with settlements.

### Taulas (illustrated on pages 1, 54-55)
Most fascinating are the *taulas*, named from the Latin word *ta(b)ula* meaning 'table'. Whereas the *talayot* is not totally unlike buildings found elsewhere (the *nuraghe* of Sardinia for example), the *taula* is unique to Menorca. It is a large, sometimes huge, slab of stone, set upright in a groove in the rock and supporting another large slab lying horizontally across it. The *taula* is always found in settlements, never far from a *talayot*, and inside a small horseshoe shaped enclosure, surrounded by standing stones, like a tiny Stonehenge. Once again, nobody knows what they were for, and the ancient writers do not mention them. It is claimed they are too tall to be altars, and the most popular suggestion is that they are idols, like totem poles in North America, symbols of gods. One scholar has suggested that they may represent bulls' heads.

### Hypostyle chambers (illustrated on page 64)
'Hypostyle chamber' describes a roof supported by pillars. These buildings, partly underground, are built up with large stones. They are roofed quite haphazardly with huge stones lying across the stone pillars, which are always much wider at the top than at the bottom.

### Navetas (illustrated on page 128)
So named by Juán Ramis y Ramis, the first Spanish writer on Menorcan prehistory, in 1818, the *naveta* is a stone-built burial chamber which resembles an upside-down boat. Hence its name, from the Latin word for boat (*navis*). The *naveta* was always built at some distance from the village.

# Flowers, birds and tortoises

Menorca is wonderfully rich in wild flowers and birds. Although having the characteristic brown appearance of Mediterranean countries during July and August, for most of the year the island's ample rainfall gives it a rich green colouring, splashed with the vivid hues of its multitude of flowers.

Left to itself, I suppose that the mastic bush, *Pistacia lentiscus*, would soon take over the whole island. You will see it everywhere — growing out of walls and blocking footpaths you want to use, covering *talayots*, trapped behind stone walls in the middle of every field. There are many other bushes and shrubs to be found, including myrtle and juniper, wild olive and fig, but very few trees. The pine is the only common real tree, especially *Pinus halepensis*, the Aleppo pine, although *Pinus pinea*, the umbrella pine, is also to be found. Mercifully the bushes are more or less contained, allowing such a variety of wayside flowers to flourish as to excite wonder and envy in the English visitor. Over a thousand species of plant have been identified on the island, and what is in flower will depend on the month of your visit. In early summer the gardener whose pride is in his gladioli will certainly see *Gladiolus communis*, its wild ancestor. Widespread and spectacular is *Hedysarum coronarium*, with red lupin-like flowers. In the same season you will see everywhere asphodel with white flowers raised high on long stems above yucca-like leaves. The pasture fields are filled with variegated thistles and walls festooned with pink *Convolvulus althaeoides*, and *Cistus*. A common 'weed' of the verges is the herb fennel, whose feathery leaves smell of aniseed, and vivid red poppies. October sees the autumn crocus whose delight is to push through the bare earth of the tracks you walk along.

In high summer the flowers are dead, but the withered seed heads of this multitude of plants feed an equal abundance of birds at this time, none more prolific than the goldfinch, while in spring and early summer the song of birds is unending wherever you walk.

The national bird might be said to be the red kite, shown on page 127. It is unmistakable, and rarely will you complete a walk without one slowly circling above your head. It is a very large bird, with wings ending in 'fingers' spread wide. From below, silhouetted, the large white patches under its wings and its deeply forked tail make it easy to identify. Seen from above when it swoops into a valley, the sun blazing down upon it, it is magnificent. Another large bird which behaves in a similar way, but is much less common, is the booted eagle. Its tail is wedge-shaped however, and it has a broad white band across the top of its wings — just the opposite of the kite, so that you need to be above it to be sure of identifying it. Most large white birds circling round pretending to be hawks will be herring gulls. You will always know when a fishing boat is coming in by the cloud of herring gulls above it. However, if a large white bird looks like a kite, but with the white and black bands beneath its wings reversed, you are having the good fortune to see an Egyptian vulture.

All the little birds you see seem to have black heads and pale bellies. This is because it is a characteristic of four very common species: blackcap, Sardinian warbler, stonechat and pied flycatcher. The stonechat is probably the easiest of the four to pick out. His back is black as well as his head, and he has a red breast, so that he looks a bit like a black robin. He loves to perch on some spike rising above the bush, and is not too timid, so that he will often sit there 'chatting' while you get a good look at him.

Crows are rare, but one that you will see is the raven, usually alone. The following are also quite common: short-toed and crested larks, alpine swifts (there are ordinary swifts too), grey and purple herons, corn buntings, kestrels, linnets, crag martins, house martins, swallows, tawny pipits (like wagtails, only brown), spotted flycatchers, red-legged partridges, house sparrows, nightingales, whinchats, rock pigeons, turtle doves.

There are several waders and ducks that you may see in the bays and lagoons, especially at S'Albufera. Cormorants are common. I once saw one at Santandría standing for ages, hanging its wings out to dry, surrounded by small children who thought it was a penguin.

I have left the best two until last. One is quite a large bird, glorious pink in colour, with a splendid crest and wings that look like a piano keyboard when it flies past. It is the hoopoe. I have met them on many of my walks, usually in pairs, and always with the same thrill of excitement. The other is the bee-eater, described on page 43.

As for the rest of the fauna, there are snails and lizards everywhere, especially in the dry-stone walls. Black beetles, butterflies and bees abound. But the really exotic creature which will delight your children is the tortoise, often seen on woodland paths.

# ⚘ Picnicking

Menorca abounds in quiet, shady, isolated, scenic spots perfect for picnicking. All the car tours and walks in this book indicate several such ideal places. Unfortunately, many of them are only accessible on foot and are not very close to bus stops. (The best places for picnics invariably tend to be well along the route of a walk, two or three miles from the bus stop. Great if you are intent upon a good walk, but too far if you are lugging a hamper.)

There are 17 picnic suggestions on the following pages. All of them are indicated on the touring map with the symbol **P**. However, since many of the picnics lie along or near the route of walks, you can pin-point their location more accurately on the appropriate large-scale *walking* map, where you will also find the symbol **P**.

All the information you need to get to these picnics is given below; 🚍: how to get there by bus; 🚗: where to park your car. Please glance over the comments before you start off on your picnic: if some walking is involved, remember to wear sensible shoes and to take a sunhat (○ = picnic in full sun.) Take along a plastic groundsheet as well, in case the ground is damp or prickly.

*Platja de Son Saura (Walk 18)*

**1  ERMITA DE SANT JOAN (Car tours 1 and 2, Walk 3; town plan pages 36-37 and map on reverse of touring map; photograph page 44)**

🚌 to Mahón. Either follow Walk 3 to the *ermita* (**40min on foot**) or take this shorter route: with your back to the War Memorial, leave the Esplanade Square by the left-hand corner and follow Sa Rovellada de Dalt as far as Carrer de Ciutadella. Cross over into Carrer Sol, take first left into Carrer Santa Victoria and continue to the junction with Carrer Cronista Riudavets. Cross over and continue along a narrow road and then a track. When you reach the main road, cross over, turn left along it for 15m/yds, and then go right along the continuation of the track. This brings you to the *ermita* shown on page 44 after **25min on foot**.
🚗 From the roundabout outside Mahón on the C721, drive down towards the port and, just before the T-junction, turn left along a minor road (Camí de Sant Joan). Park beside the church after 0.75km/0.5mi. **No walking.**

**2  CALA DE SANT ESTEVE ('ST STEPHEN'S CREEK'; Car tour 1, Walk 4; map on reverse of touring map; drawing page 18)**

🚌 to Es Castell; then follow notes for motorists below. **40min on foot.**
🚗 Drive from Mahón past Es Castell. Keep straight on at the Sol del Este/Sant Lluís crossroads, and turn right just short of the army base along a narrow road. Follow the road round the *cala* and park at the end. Climb up beside the old tower shown on page 18 to gain access to the coast, and picnic anywhere you like. Allow up to **10min on foot**. You will find some shade at the Marlborough Redoubt and the Torre d'en Penjat. (See also Picnic 17; it is close by.)

**3  ES GRAU (Car tours 1 and 2, Walk 2; map page 41; photograph of similar setting page 43)**

🚌 from Mahón to Es Grau; then see notes for motorists below.
🚗 Drive along the Fornells road from Mahón and in 0.75km take the first road on the right for Es Grau. Park by the beach. There are two pine-shaded picnic places near this magnificent beach. One is among the trees which border the beach itself. For the second, allow up to **20min on foot**: walk to the end of the beach and follow a path up the cliff. Turn left at the top and descend a track to a little valley, where you will find an open space among trees. For a short walk, follow the track round to the right, up out of the valley, and turn right at the top, by a wall. Then follow the track back towards Es Grau (seen ahead). Turn right at a junction, go down into a valley, then climb steeply, to regain your outgoing route. Keep straight on to return to the beach.

**4  CALA MORELL (Car tour 2, Walk 23; map page 130; photograph page 132; drawing opposite)**

🚌 mini-bus to Cala Morell; then see notes for motorists below.
🚗 to Cala Morell; park in the car park on the right. The rocks may be too crowded, but the area around the caves, described in Walk 23, should be quieter (allow up to **5min on foot**). If you explore a little you should find somewhere that you will have more or less to yourself.

**5  TALATÍ DE DALT (Car tour 2, Walks 7 and 8; map on reverse of touring map; photographs pages 1, 60-61, 65)**

🚗 Leave Mahón along the C721. In 4km turn south along a metalled lane for 0.5km, and park in the lay-by near the 'Taula de Talatí' sign. Cross the wall using the protruding stone steps (*botador*) and follow the

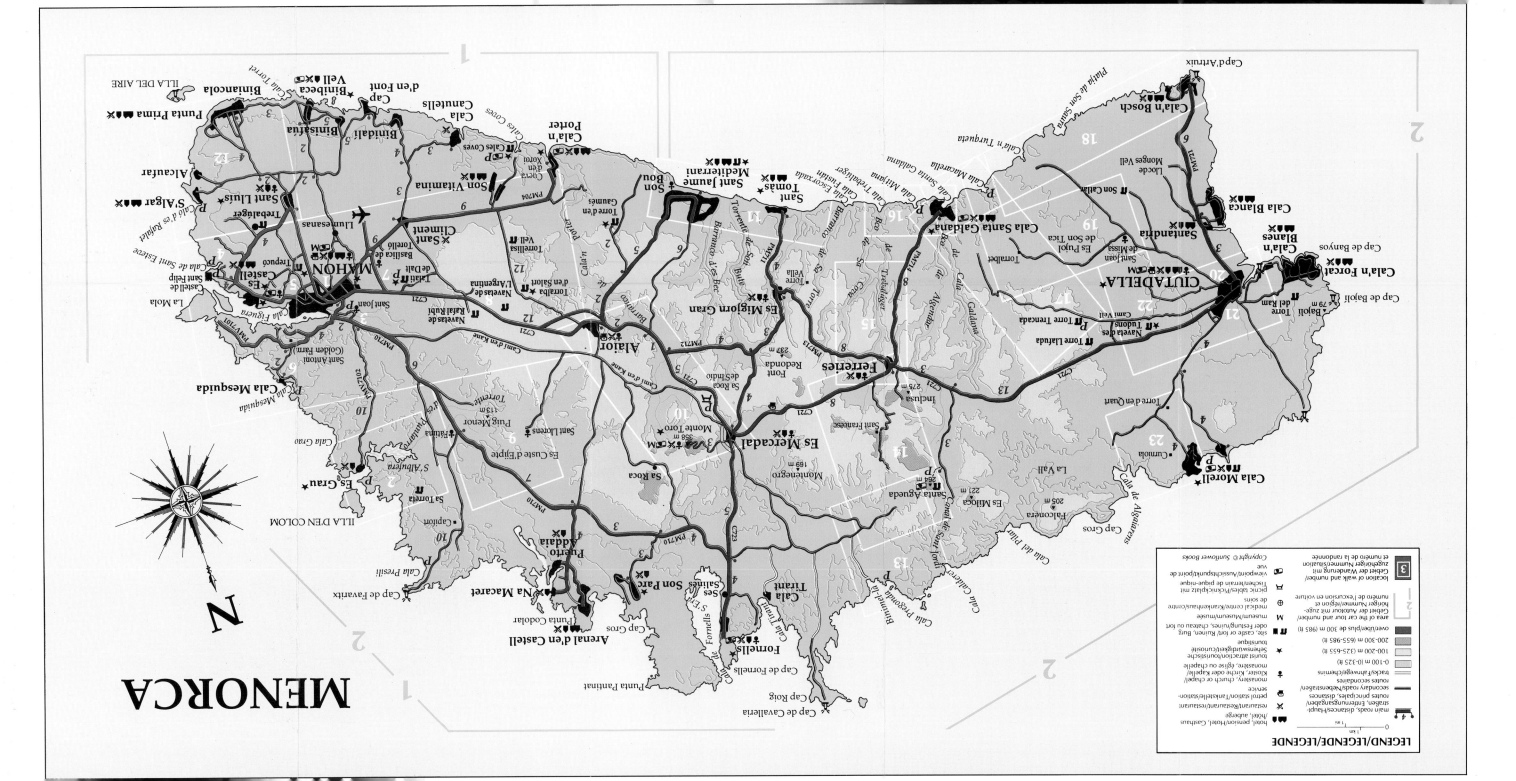

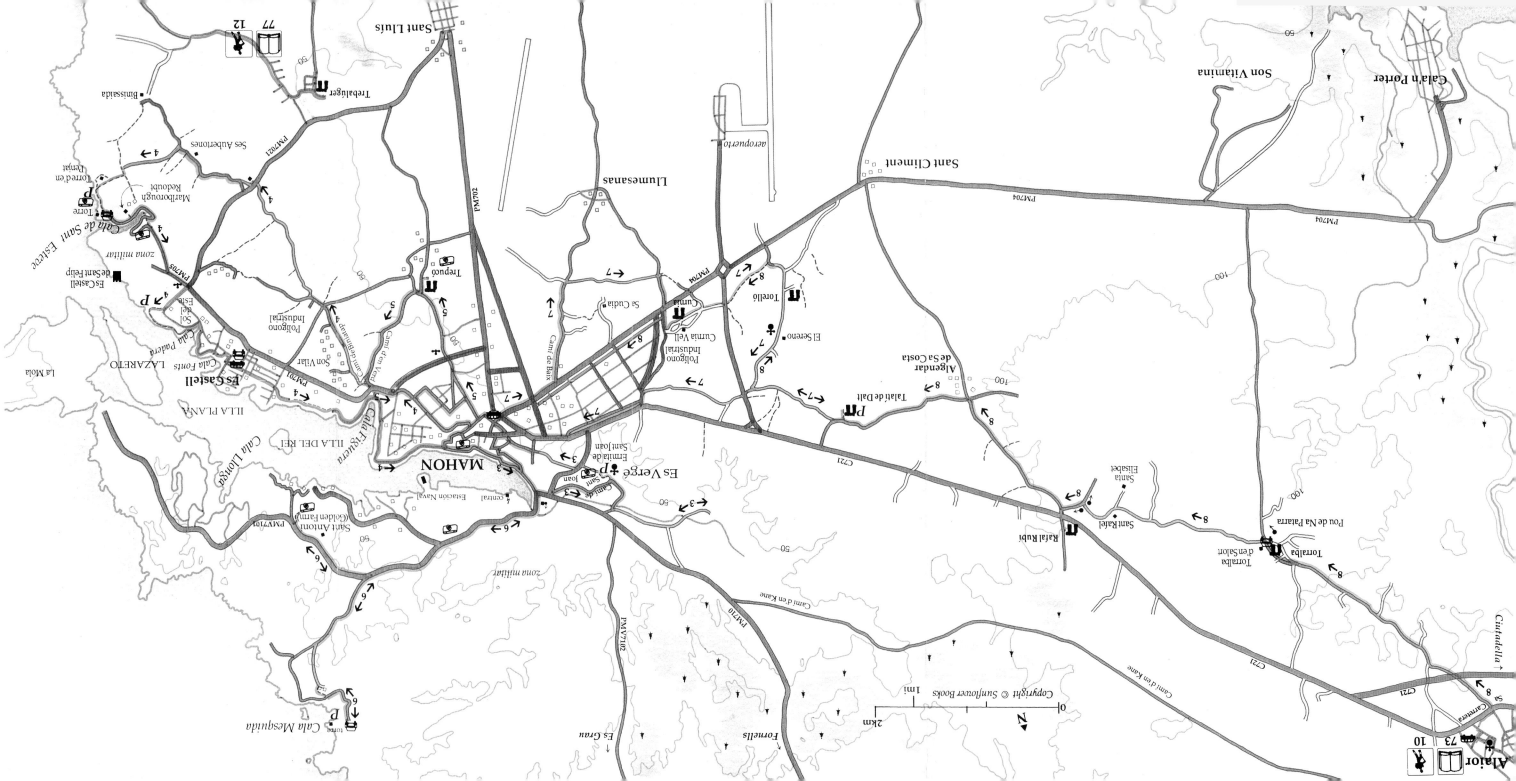

track to the site of this prehistoric village, which is usually quiet enough for a peaceful picnic in romantic surroundings. The notes for Walks 7 and 8 tell you more about the site.

### 6 CALA MESQUIDA (Car tour 1, Walk 6; map on reverse of touring map ○)

🚗 Park at the rear of the splendid, usually quiet, Cala Mesquida. Picnic on the beach, or explore the cliffs.

### 7 CALA PRESILI (Car tour 1; see touring map ○)

🚗 Drive from Mahón towards Fornells along the PM710, and turn right in 9km along a road signposted 'Fo. de Favaritx'. Park at the end of the road, by the entrance to the lighthouse (at the KM2 marker). Allowing **20min on foot**, walk back 0.7km/0.5mi to the small 100m-marker with the number 3. Turn left here along a rocky track, and in seven minutes turn left at junction. Five minutes later you reach the small beach.

### 8 SANTA AGUEDA (Car tour 2; touring map and map page 86)

🚗 Turn north off the C721 some 3km northwest of Ferreries, towards the hill of Santa Agueda, and in 3km park beside the former village school. To the right of the school a gate gives onto a path which is a Roman road, still partly paved. In **5min** you reach a quiet shady spot with stones to sit on; **30min** brings you to the top of the hill, where the Romans had a fortress and a Moorish king had his summer palace.

### 9 SA ROCA DE S'INDIO (Car tour 1; see touring map 🎌 ○)

🚗 Park 2km south of Es Mercadal on the C721 to Alaior. This is Menorca's only organised picnic site, named for the rock opposite it, which resembles a Red Indian chief. Tables and benches, but no shade.

### 10 CALA MITJANA (Car tour 2, Walk 16; map pages 96-97)

🚌 Cala Santa Galdana. Turn left and cross to far side of the beach. Climb a flight of steps to the top of the cliff. Turn left along the road, and after 100m/yds follow the directions for motorists below. Allow **35min on foot**.

🚗 Drive to Cala Santa Galdana. On reaching the roundabout outside the town, take the third exit (signposted 'Hotel Gavilanes'). Drive to within 200m of the end, and park when you come to a parking area on the left. Before setting off, you may wish to walk to the viewing platform on your right for a magnificent view of the bay. Then turn down Carrer Camí d'es Cavalls and continue along a short

*Capades de Moro at Cala Morell (Picnic 4, Walk 23)*

*Old tower above St Stephen's Creek (Picnic 2, Walk 4)*

track through a gateway. After 20m/yds, when the path divides, turn left towards some houses. In five minutes go through a gap in the wall and bear right. Two minutes later go over a crossing track, and after a similar interval walk diagonally to the right across an open space, to join a wider track. Bear right again and keep on this track, ignoring all minor paths and tracks to left and right until you descend to the *cala* after **15min on foot**.

**11 CALA MACARELLA (Car tour 2, Walks 17-19; map pages 96-97; photograph page 95)**

🚌 to Cala Santa Galdana, then follow notes for motorists below and allow **40min on foot**.

🚗 Drive to Cala Santa Galdana. On reaching the roundabout outside the town, take the second exit and drive down to the bay; there is a large car park on the right. Now allow **40min on foot**. Follow the first section of Walk 18 from Cala Santa Caldana to Cala Macarella, using the notes on pages 105-106. Cafeteria Susy is open from late April to October.

**12 CALA PREGONDA (map page 81 O)**

🚗 Enter Es Mercadal by the first street on the left if you are coming from Ferreries, the last on the right (beyond the windmill) if you are coming from Alaior, and after 50m bear left following 'Playas Costa Norte'. You leave the town along a narrow country road. Ignore the first road on the right, but after 6.5km turn sharply right for Binimel-là. After 0.5km turn left along a wide dirt road. In 1km pass through a narrow gateway, and after a similar distance turn left down a track to the beach. Park here, being careful to avoid soft sand. Now allow **25min on foot**. Walk to the left along the beach. Leave it before you get to the end, forking diagonally left on a path between low bushes. Make for a wall ahead. Climb over the wall, and follow a wide track across the next beach, and on to another wall. Go through a gap in the corner, and follow the path diagonally ahead towards white cliffs. Cross some sand dunes, another beach, more dunes, and climb towards one more wall. Make for the last concrete pole supporting power lines, and go through an iron gate. Turn right on a wide track above the beach, finally descending along a path signposted 'Paso a la playa visitantes' to the beach.

**13 TORRE TRENCADA (Car tour 2, Walk 17; map pages 96-97 ⛩)**

🚗 Coming from Ciutadella on the C721, turn right shortly before the KM39 marker along a country lane signposted 'Torre Trencada'. Turn left at the T-junction, and after 2km park in a small car park. Follow the signposted path to the site of the prehistoric settlement of Torre Trencada (**8min on foot**), with its megalithic picnic table set beneath ancient olive trees in the middle of a prehistoric village.

### 14 CALO D'ES RAFALET (Walk 12; map page 77)

🚌 to S'Algar; then see notes for motorists below.

🚗 Drive to S'Algar. Turn right as you enter the resort, and park in the car park on your right. Allow **40min on foot**. Walk down to the sea front (photograph pages 78-79) and turn left. At the end of the sea front, walk past a wall, turn left, and walk uphill beside it. Continue with the sea to your right, up to the top of the hill. Use the *botador* (stile) to climb over the wall here, turn left and walk parallel with the creek, to the end of a long field. Turn right, and go downhill to a gap in the wall. Cross another field to leave through the gap at the wall's end. Turn right along a track, and in 20m/yds turn right again. As the track turns left, look out for a gap in the wall on your right after 20m/yds (waymarked with a red arrow on a tree). Turn right and follow the path along a dried-up river bed to the end, where you will find a shady picnic area. Follow the path on to a tiny sandy beach and lovely little cove, overlooked from the rocks on your left.

### 15 CALES COVES from Cala'n Porter (Car tour 1; touring map)

🚌 to Cala'n Porter. From the bus stop allow **35min on foot**. Bear left and walk uphill along the main street to the cliff edge, following signs for the 'Cova d'en Xoroi'. Now refer to notes for motorists below.

🚗 Drive to Cala'n Porter. Do not take the road on the right down to the beach, but drive straight through the town to the cliff edge. Park where convenient and allow about **15min on foot**. Turn left along the cliff edge, and follow any of the several paths parallel with the sea which is rarely more than 12m/yds away. In ten minutes you will be looking over the end of the creek. The path turns left here, parallel now with the *cala*. In about five minutes you will come to a place where you have a good view of the prehistoric caves in the cliffs opposite. Behind you the pine wood offers several open shady areas just right for picnicking on a hot day.

### 16 CALES COVES from Son Vitamina (Car tour 1; touring map ○)

🚌 Take the Cala'n Porter bus from Mahón, but alight at Son Vitamina and allow **35min on foot**. Walk up the side road until you reach an open area from which radiate a track and two roads; then see notes for motorists below.

🚗 Drive to Son Vitamina on the road to Cala'n Porter. Park in the open space at the entrance to the village and allow **30min on foot**. Walk down the track on your right, to arrive at a picturesque creek in whose cliffs are many prehistoric caves.

### 17 FORT ST PHILIP (Car tour 1, Walk 4, see map on reverse of touring map ○)

🚌 to Es Castell and **25min on foot**. Walk back to the main road, turn left and walk beside it as far as the Sol del Este crossroads. Turn left and walk towards the sea until, just before the road bends left, there is a gap in the wall on your right. Now refer to notes for motorists below.

🚗 Drive from Mahón past Es Castell as far as the Sol del Este crossroads. Turn left and park just before the road bends left, near to a gap in the wall on your right. Now allow **5min on foot**. Go through the gap in the wall, and follow the track to your right. There are exceptional views of the harbour mouth, La Mola and Lazareto Island. Explore the remains of Fort St Philip as far as the *zona militar*. (Note that Picnic 2 is nearby, on the south side of St Stephen's Creek.)

# ❊ Touring

There are many car hire firms on Menorca, or you can reserve one via your travel agent or holiday firm at home. Charges can vary considerably, so shop around. The cheapest deal does not necessarily mean the worst car. Be certain to ask for and get 'Collision Damage Waiver', otherwise you will be liable for any repair bill for the car that you incur. On which topic, a word of warning. If you are only used to right-hand drive cars and driving on the left, then collecting your totally unfamiliar car at the airport, after dark (when you forgot you had to drive and so had a few drinks on the flight), can be unnerving.

Always check your vehicle in advance and point out any existing dents, scratches etc. Ask for all the conditions and insurance cover in writing, in English. Check to make sure you have a sound spare tyre and all the necessary tools. Be sure to get the office and the after-hours telephone numbers of the hire firm and carry them with you. If you are not 100% happy about the car, don't take it. Finally, make a note of exactly what you are signing for, if you pay by credit card.

The two car tours will take you to the majority of the notable places on the island (indicated with a ★ in the touring notes and on the touring map). The touring notes are quite brief. I concentrate instead on the 'logistics' of touring and the possibilities for nearby **countryside**

**picnics** and **walks**. (Usually further historical notes can be found in the text with the relevant walk.)

**The large fold-out touring map is designed to be held out opposite the touring notes** and contains all the information you will need outside the towns. Town plans of Mahón and Ciutadella, showing exits for motorists, are on pages 36-37 and 114-115 respectively. **Remember to allow plenty of time for visits**. The times given in the tours are actual driving times, and no allowance has been made for time spent sightseeing. The distances quoted in the notes are cumulative kilometres from the departure point. A key **to the symbols** used in the touring notes is on the touring map.

There very few tarmac roads apart from those in the two tours, and they are for the most part single lane carriageways with passing places, which is why I have avoided them. The exceptions are the new, quite wide roads, sometimes with signs reading 'ZONA D'ORDENACIO DE EXPLOTACIONS DE MENORCA CONSELLERIA D'AGRICULTURA I PESCA GOVERN BALEAR' and names beginning with 'Camí de ...', followed by the name of a farm. *These are a trap for the unwary visitor.* Financed by the Ministry of Agriculture, they provide a modern link for the farmers with the main roads, and almost invariably they stop at the farm gate. In practically every instance they are 'no through roads'.

**All motorists should read the country code on page 10 and go quietly in the countryside.**

*Car tour 1: The lovely fishing village of Fornells prospered under the protection of its 16th-century hillside tower.*

# 1 EASTERN MENORCA

**Mahón/Maó • Favaritx • Arenal d'en Castell • Fornells • Es Mercadal • Monte Toro • Alaior • Torralba • Cala'n Porter • (Cales Coves) • Sant Climent • Binibeca Vell • Sant Lluís • Es Castell • Mahón/Maó**

*129km/81mi; about 4 hours' driving*

**On route:** Picnics (see pages 15-19) 1, 2, 3, 6, 7, 9, 12, 14, 15, 16, 17; Walks 1, 2, 3, 4, 5, 6, 7, 8, 9, 10, 12, 13

*The roads are generally good and adequately wide, although occasionally bumpy. There are petrol stations in Mahón (Maó), on the PM710 two kilometres before the Arenal turn-off, and in Alaior. **Important:** although the driving time is only four hours, allow an entire day if you want to visit all the tourist attractions.*

A modern highway, the C721, runs across Menorca connecting the capital Mahón (Maó) with the second largest town and former capital, Ciutadella. On it lie the three next largest towns of the island — Alaior, Es Mercadal and Ferreries. Just outside Mahón on this road there is a large roundabout, which has been taken as the nominal start and finish of this tour, although being circular it can be joined and left wherever is convenient.

Coming from **Mahón★** (♣🏔🏠✕🍽🚐🗺M; Walks 1, 3, 5-7; notes page 33), turn right at the roundabout and follow the road downhill towards the port. At the bottom of the hill turn left in the direction of Fornells along the PM710 (a right turn leads to Cala Mesquida; Picnic 6, Walk 6). This is the beginning of the Camí d'en Kane (Kane's Road), built early in the 18th century by the first British lieutenant-governor of Menorca, Sir Richard Kane, to link Ciutadella in the north with Port Mahón, replacing the earlier road built by the Romans. You will see a memorial to him on your right soon after the start of the road. This first stretch necessitated the draining of marshes, resulting in the creation of the rich agricultural land you see on your left. The nearby Camí de Sant Joan would take you to the setting for Picnic 1 and Walk 3.

Almost at once pass a road on the right to Es Grau★, a tiny resort with a large beach (Picnic 3, Walk 2). Soon the Camí d'en Kane bears away to the left. However you keep straight on, following signs for Fornells. The road continues in a northwesterly direction through a beautiful countryside of lightly-wooded low hills. Some 2.8km beyond the Camí d'en Kane turning, ignore another turn-off on the left, and continue in the direction of Fornells for another kilometre, when you will pass on your right the little church ('*ermita*') shown on page 68. It is dedicated to Our Lady of Fátima, and Walk 9 begins here.

Another road now goes to the right. It is signposted 'F(ar)o (lighthouse) de Favaritx'. Turn along here. At first the road is very straight as it crosses flat terrain, passing the estate of Capifort, before winding between low green hills, to end at the lighthouse at **Cape Favaritx** (17.5km). There is car parking here and, 0.7km back along the road, a track on the left brings you in 12 minutes' walking to the beach of Cala Presili (Picnic 7).

Returning to the PM710, turn right to drive through increasingly wooded scenery. In 6.5km you arrive at a crossroads. Three resorts lie at the end of the road to the right: Arenal d'en Castell, Na Macaret and Puerto Addaia. Arenal probably has the most to offer you, although Puerto Addaia can provide a boat trip along a charming *cala*, the third longest in Menorca. All three are well signposted: turn right and, when you come to another crossroads, go left for Arenal, straight on for Na Macaret, or right for Addaia. The long, curved beach at **Arenal d'en Castell** (36km 🏖🏖🏖✕) is one of the best on the island (*arenal* means 'sandy beach'). The small seaside village of Na Macaret (🏖✕) is one of the oldest holiday resorts on Menorca. Puerto Addaia (🏖✕) overlooks the harbour. When in the mid-18th century John Armstrong wrote the first English guidebook to Menorca, he described Addaia as the most exquisite place on the island.

Again return to the PM710, turn right and follow signs for Fornells. In 3km you will pass the turn-off right for Son Parc★ (🏖✕ and Menorca's only golf course). After 6.5km you will reach one more crossroads at the junction with the C723. Turn right. For 4km the C723 runs beside the

*Typical farm, surrounded by flowers and dry-stone walls*

second largest *cala* on Menorca. Remote from Ciutadella and Mahón, it was once a favourite anchorage of Mediterranean pirates. As a result no Menorcans would live there. In 1591 the governor decided that the time had come to do something about the pirates, and a start was made on fortifying the entrance to the harbour. The ruins of that fortress will be seen if you walk towards the harbour mouth. Under its protection the lovely fishing village of **Fornells★** (51km ♦▲✕⌨; photograph pages 20-21) grew up. You can see on the Isla Sarganta in the bay a tower built by the British to provide crossfire and, on the headland overlooking the village and harbour entrance, a second tower.

Drive back beside the *cala* to the crossroads and turn right. Follow a country lane for just over 4km, when you will pass on your right a wide dirt road. It leads to the beach of Binimel-là (parking for Walk 13 and the turn-off for Picnic 12). In 0.5km turn sharp left for Es Mercadal; you will pass one tarmac road on the left en route. As you enter **Es Mercadal** (66km ♦▲✕) look out for the road on the left signposted '**Monte Toro**'. A short, steep, winding drive will take you to the summit★ of the mountain (69km ♦✕⌨M; photograph page 71). At 358m/1175ft, this is the highest point on Menorca, from where the whole of the island can be seen. It is also the high point of Walk 10. Its name probably dates back to the time of the Moorish occupation, deriving from the Arabic word *tor* meaning 'mountain'. However the fact that *toro* means 'bull' in Spanish has caused a curious legend to arise. It is claimed that the bull in question hewed with its horns a statue of the Virgin Mary out of rock, and that the name of the mountain commemorates this miracle.

Return to Es Mercadal and, on reaching the C721, turn left towards Mahón. Shortly after leaving the town you will pass the electricity substation on the right, and then at the top of the hill you will find on the left the island's only organised picnic site, **Sa Roca de S'Indío** (⌂; Picnic 9). The rock opposite bears an uncanny resemblance to a Hollywood Red Indian chief.

Carry on; approaching **Alaior** (80km ♦✕⌨), ignore the bypass and bear left to drive through the town. Just before the end of the town, turn right along a road signposted 'Cala En Porter'. This is the start of Walk 8. After 3km you will arrive at the important megalithic site of **Torralba d'en Salort★** (83km ⛏). You will find more about Alaior in the notes for Walk 10, and about Torralba

*The Cave of Xoroi, a bar and night-club, is built in a prehistoric cave dwelling at the end of Cala'n Porter.*

in those for Walk 8. The road bends to your right now, and in 2.5km you will see over to your right the *talayot* of Torrellisa Vell (**IT**). A kilometre beyond is a T-junction.

Turn right at this junction and you will shortly arrive at **Cala'n Porter** (91.5km ▲▲▲✕📷; Picnic 15). The fairly large holiday resort is built high above a fine beach. Set in the cliff at the end of the *cala* is the **Cave of Xoroi★**, shown above. Leave Cala'n Porter by the road you came in on and, when you reach the Alaior junction, keep ahead towards Sant Climent and Mahón.

***Recommended diversion.*** If you have time for a short walk (1h return), after 0.5km take the road on the right signposted 'Son Vitamina'. Park in the open space at the entrance to Son Vitamina (94.5km ▲▲▲✕) and walk down the rough track which ends at the head of one of the prettiest of all the *calas* and the impressive troglodytic site of Cales Coves★ (**IT**📷; Picnic 16).

The main tour makes straight for **Sant Climent** (98.5km ✕). At the end of the village turn right (by a restaurant). Notice the stone seats along the walls now. They were made to accommodate spectators of the trotting races, still popular in Menorca, which were formerly held along here. In 2.5km a road to the right leads to Cala Canutells, but unless you want to make this detour, keep straight on to **Binidalí**, and turn left when you reach the sea.

*Tower near Alcaufar (Walk 12); see also photograph pages 78-79.*

What follows is the nearest you can get on Menorca to a coastal road. It is impossible to give detailed directions — there are so many tiny streets as you drive from one resort to the next. It scarcely matters which streets you go along, you cannot get lost. Just keep heading southeast, and as close to the coast as you can, following signs for Cap d'en Font, Binisafúa, Binibeca, Biniancola and Punta Prima — which you will pass, in that order, in the course of the next 10.5km. Do drive carefully and slowly through the resorts. One that you should take time to explore is **Binibeca Vell★** (▲✕🖼). It was one of the first *urbanizaciones* and was designed to replicate a typical Menorcan fishing village (a curious conceit, since there is no such thing; you have already seen Menorca's only fishing village — Fornells — and it is nothing like this!). It has been described, not inaccurately, as the ideal setting for a folklore film. At the southeast tip of the island is **Punta Prima** (113km ▲▲▲✕). Here you turn left and head for Sant Lluís, some 5km distant. Halfway along, a road on the right leads to S'Algar and Picnic 14.

**Sant Lluís★** (118.5 🛉▲✕) is the starting point for Walk 12, where you can read more about its origins. On leaving, turn right at the crossroads towards Es Castell. As you pass the village of Trebalúger on the right, look for its prominent *talayot*. In 4km you will reach a crossroads near a cemetery. Until 1782 the road to the right led to the mighty Fort St Philip. Take it now to enjoy Picnic 2, or cross over for Picnic 17; otherwise turn left. You skirt to the left of **Es Castell** (123km 🛉▲▲▲✕🖼; described in the notes for Walk 4). Soon the road bends and dips to Cala Figuera. Turn right here, down to Mahón's harbour. Turn left and drive the full length of the harbour road. At the end, keep left and, at the next junction, turn left, to climb to the roundabout where the tour began (129km).

26

Ciutadella • Cala Santa Galdana • Es Migjorn Gran • Sant Tomàs • Sant Jaume Mediterrani • Alaior • Mahón • Es Grau • Es Mercadal • Ferreries • Ciutadella

*Distance: 150km/93mi; about 4 hours' driving*

**On route:** *Picnics (see pages 15-19) 1, 3, 4, 5, 7, 8, 10, 11, 12, 13; Walks 2, 3, 8, 10, 11, 13, 14, 15, 16, 17, 18, 19, 20, 21, 22, 23*
*The roads are generally adequately wide and well surfaced, although the road into Sant Jaume is bumpy. There are petrol stations in Ciutadella, Alaior, and just outside Es Mercadal. Note that there is a speed restriction on the Camí d'en Kane.* **Important:** *although the driving time is only four hours, allow a full day to visit all the tourist attractions.*

T he ancient and fascinating city of Ciutadella has been chosen for the starting point of this tour, out of consideration for the many tourists settled in the resorts of the northwest of the island. Since the tour is circular it can, of course, be joined and left wherever is convenient.

**Ciutadella★** (♦♠▲✕♥☞M) is the starting point for Walks 20-22; see notes page 113. Leave the town along the Camí de Maó, the beginning of the C721 highway to Mahón (Maó). After 4km look out for the **Naveta d'es Tudons★** (♟) on your right. It is clearly signposted and there is ample parking. A visit to this monument, shown on page 128, is *de rigueur,* if only because of its claim to be the oldest roofed building in Europe. It is visited on Walk 22, where you can read more about it. At 5.3km, near the KM39 marker, turn right along a road signposted '**Torre Trencada'.** Turn left at the T-junction, leave your car in the small parking area, and follow the path to the interesting prehistoric settlement visited on Walk 17 and Picnic 13. Then return to the C721 and turn right. In 2km, a farm track on the right leads to yet another important prehistoric site, that of Torre Llafuda (♟). Just over 5km further along, you could take a detour up a minor road on the left, towards a hill with famous historical associations — Santa Agueda (264m/870ft; ♟☞). A short walk would take you to the settings for Picnic 8.

The main tour continues on the C721 towards Ferreries. In 2.5km a road on the right takes you to beautiful **Cala Santa Galdana★** (29km ♠▲✕☞; photograph pages 28-29; Picnics 10 and 11, Walks 16-18; Shorter walk 19-2). When you reach the roundabout at the resort's entrance, take the last exit (signposted 'Hotel Gavilanes') and drive to the end, where you will have a panoramic view over the bay.

Return to the C721 and turn right towards Ferreries. In 0.5km you come to another junction on the right, at the entrance to Ferreries. Leave the C721 here, and drive to **Es Migjorn Gran** (44.5km ✚▲✕), a small town founded in 1763. Turn right on the far side of town, passing through a region rich in megalithic monuments (mostly not visible from the road). The road ends at a long beach of silver sand, at **Sant Tomàs★** (48.5km ▲▲▲✕; Walk 11).

Return to Es Migjorn and keep straight on towards Es Mercadal. In 3km turn right towards Alaior and Mahón. In 4km you rejoin the C721. Turn right and, after 1km, take the next road on the right to **Sant Jaume Mediter-rani★** (66.5km **▮**▲▲▲✕). It has a long beach separated from lines of villas by a wide marsh. Turn left and drive to the far end of the resort — **Son Bou** (✚), then turn right for the beach and car park. This is where Walk 11 starts, and in the notes you can read more about the area.

Return to the T-junction, turn right and head back towards Alaior. After 5km turn right and, in 2km, keep left at a fork, to reach the largest of the cyclopean townships, **Torre d'en Gaumés★** (74km **▮**; drawing page 64).

Drive back to the Son Bou/Alaior road and turn right. In 2.5km you will be back at the C721 just as it reaches **Alaior** (79km ✚✕🖳), the third largest town on Menorca. If you wish to see it, ignore the bypass and drive almost to the far side of the town, where you will see a road on the right signposted 'Cala En Porter'. If you drive a short distance along here, you should find room to park beside the road. Walks 8 and 10 start here, and the notes for Walk 10 will tell you a little about the town. Otherwise carry on along the C721 as it bypasses the town, heading for Mahón. On the way you will pass four *navetas:* two

*Cala Santa Galdana: Menorcans regard it as their most beautiful resort and bitterly regret its 'urbaniza-ción'. There is no saint named 'Galdana'; the name is a corruption of the Moorish 'Guad-al-Ana' ('Barranco of St Anne'), after whom an adjacent farm is named (Car tour 2; Walks 16-18; Shorter walk 19-2).*

on the right at L'Argentina, and two on the left at Rafal Rubí (all signposted and visible from the road). After 8km turn right on a minor road to the prehistoric site of **Talatí de Dalt**★ (87.5km ▯; Picnic 5; Walks 7 and 8; notes page 60; photographs pages 1, 60-61, 65).

Returning to the main road, continue to a large round-about at the edge of **Mahón** (described in Walk 1). Turn left towards the port, and left again at the T-junction at the bottom of the hill. (A minor road on the left just before this junction leads through market gardens to the Ermita de Sant Joan ♱; Picnic 1 and Walk 3; photograph page 44.) In 0.75km take the road on the right to **Es Grau**★ (100km ▲✕; Picnic 3; Walk 2). Just as you reach this charming resort and its large and attractive beach, there is a turning to the left. Pull off the road here to admire the sea-water lagoon and nature reserve of S'Albufera.

Go back to the PM710 and turn right towards Fornells but, after 1.5km, turn left along the Camí d'en Kane (note the speed restriction). This road, described in Walk 3, affords pleasant driving through a rural landscape north of Alaior. You rejoin the C721 just short of Es Mercadal: turn right along the C721. You pass two market towns founded after the Reconquest: the first is **Es Mercadal** (126km ♱▲✕). The last street you pass on the right (by the windmill) leads to Walk 13 and Picnic 12. Just before the C721 (🚏) enters **Ferreries** (134km ♱▲✕), you pass a minor road on the right which is on the route of Walk 14; like Walk 15, it starts in Ferreries. After 150km you arrive back at Ciutadella, from where you have the easiest access to Walks 19 and 23, as well as Picnic 4.

# ❀ Walking

The walks in this book cover a good cross-section of the island. I have tried to choose walks which take you to places of interest. In some cases that will be historical or archaeological. In others it will be a beautiful, remote beach or particularly appealing scenery. There are walks to suit every taste from short strolls to rambles over 20 kilometres long. For a selection of *very* short walks, see the picnic suggestions on pages 16 to 19.

To choose a walk that appeals to you, you might begin by looking at the touring map between pages 16 and 17. Here you can see at a glance the overall terrain, the roads, and the location of the walks. Flipping through the book, you will see that there is at least one photograph for every walk. Having selected one or two potential excursions from the map and the photographs, turn to the relevant walk. At the top of the page you will find planning information: distance/time, grade, equipment, and transport details.

When you are on your walk, you will find that the text begins with an introduction and then quickly turns to a detailed description of the route. The large-scale maps (all 1:40,000) have been specially annotated to show important landmarks, and the following symbols are used:

| | | | |
|---|---|---|---|
| ▨▨▨ | main road on the touring map | 🚌🚏 | bus stop/car parking place |
| ▬▬ | secondary road on the touring road | 👁 | best views |
| ═══ | track, trail, or wide path | *100* | height in metres |
| - - - | path or steps | **P** | picnic place (see pages 15-19) |
| ← | main walking route | ⋔ ∩ | prehistoric site/cave |
| ⇐ | alternative route | □□▫□ | settlement |
| | | ■ | specific building referred to in the text |

Times are given for reaching certain points in the walk. Note: I walk at an average speed of 4km/h (2.5mph), but far from consistently. I gallop along on the flat, but crawl like a tortoise up hills. *Do* compare your pace with mine on one of the short walks, before doing a long hike. Remember, the times do not take into account any stops (other than for getting your breath back on hills). If you are catching a bus, allow plenty of time.

# Nuisances

While there are large **dogs** on the island, they are always tied up. You will come across a few small ones, not tied up, that continue to bark until they have seen you off their patch. In my experience, these have proved harmless. The few **snakes** on the island are also harmless. The only real nuisance on Menorca is the **mastic bush** (Pistacia lentiscus), which flourishes on the dry-stone walls and threatens to render impassable just about every walled-in track on the island. You should not have too much difficulty with the routes described in this book.

# What to take

These walks are not strenuous or dangerous. You are not likely to get lost nor, despite the feeling of isolation you will often have, are you ever likely to be very far away from the nearest town. Nonetheless it is worth giving some thought to what to take with you. **Footwear**, for example. I have always recommended well worn-in walking boots, for the protection they give to the ankles. But they do have drawbacks; they are hot and heavy in summer, and they may cause blisters. While preparing this Second edition I experimented with the new walking/sports sandals and was won over to them for summer walking. They were as successful in torrential rain as on hot, dry days. Of course, they, too, have their drawbacks. You get little stones under your feet, but they are quickly and easily removed. And your feet get dirty (and wet, if it is raining); but they wash and dry more easily than socks. The only real problem occurs on a few occasions when you are ploughing through brambles, when your feet could be badly torn. Then boots may be preferable. On those occasions you will also need long trousers. Beach sandals are *not* suitable for walking. Take a bandage, in case you do put your ankle out. In summer you will need a long-sleeved shirt for **protection against the sun**, and for the same reason a sunhat and long trousers. If the walk includes a beach, and many do, take a towel, swimwear and sun cream. Have **waterproof clothing** if it looks like rain, especially outside summer. You will need a **small rucksack**, band-aids for blisters, up-to-date bus timetables, and **water**. A whistle and torch are always advisable. Bird-lovers should try to have light-weight binoculars. For each walk in the book, the minimum equipment is listed. Use your good judgement to modify my equipment list according to the season!

# 1  A WALKABOUT TOUR OF MAHON

See town plan on pages 36-37; see also illustrations on pages 52, 56

**Distance:** 2.5km/1.5mi; 1h30min                    **Grade:** easy

**Equipment:** comfortable shoes of any sort, sunhat, raingear

**How to get there and return:** 🚌 or 🚗 to/from the Plaça de S'Esplanada in Mahón (bus station and underground car park)

I suppose the people of Menorca and Malta will never agree whether the Grand Harbour at Valletta or Port Mahón is the finest harbour in the Mediterranean. That the Royal Navy settled in Valletta in the 19th and 20th centuries was due entirely to the decision of Admiral Lord Nelson. Cynics argue that his choice of Valletta was itself entirely due to the fact that Malta was considerably closer to the court of Naples where Lady Hamilton's husband was British ambassador. For a century before that decision was made, Port Mahón had been the home of the British Mediterranean fleet.

**The walk begins** in the Plaça de S'Esplanada. This is the largest and most attractive of a number of squares in Mahón, or Maó as it is often called now. This square is the terminus for all the buses which serve the town. An 'esplanade' being the open space between a citadel and the first houses of the town, the name is very appropriate, for on the west side the square is overlooked by the barracks of the Spanish Regiment of Artillery. The tall monument in front of the barracks which dominates the square is dedicated to the memory of all those who gave their lives for Spain in the Civil War.

Stand with your back to the monument and face east. Walk to the street which leads away from the far right hand corner of the square. This is the Carrer de Ses Moreres. Since you will leave this street by turning right, perhaps you should cross over now and walk along the right-hand side. You can come back on the other side at the end of your tour, but crossing now will give you the opportunity to inspect the bust of Dr Orfila outside no 13, which was his birthplace. Mateu J Orfila (1787-1853) became Professor of Chemistry in the Medical Faculty of the University of Paris, and began the systematic study of poisons. He is regarded as the father of forensic medicine. This street is dedicated to him.

Ignore the street on your right called Cós de Gràcia, and walk the length of Ses Moreres until the crossroads. Here turn right. Mahón is built on a not inconsiderable hill above the harbour. The descent is in two stages. This is the first, along Carrer Bastió and down the Costa d'en

## About the town

The harbour at Mahón is three and a half miles in length, the longest and deepest of a number of fine harbours on the island. Although the harbourage here is excellent, being bordered by high cliffs it is somewhat inaccessible. However there was one place where a small cove cut into the cliff, and a path ran down to the sea. At the top of the cliff overlooking this cove a fortified village was built in ancient times.

One of the first people on record to have anchored his ships here was a Carthaginian general in 206BC. His name was Mago, brother of the famous Hannibal. When the Romans named the village Municipium Flavianum Magontanum, they may have been naming it after him. Later it was to give its name to mayonnaise!

After the Romans, Vandals and Byzantines in turn occupied Mahón until the coming of the Moors, and in 902AD Menorca became part of the Emirate of Cordova. The Moors wanted a harbour nearer to Spain, and built their capital at Ciutadella, but it was here at Mahón that the Reconquest of Menorca began.

On 5th January 1287 King Alfonso III of Aragón sailed into the harbour with twenty ships and landed on the Isla del Rei ('the King's Island', illustrated on page 52). After defeating the Moors, Alfonso resettled the island with Catalans. At various times in the future more and more settlers came from that eastern province of Spain, so that the language of the island came to be a form of Catalan known as 'Menorquín'. (This has been strongly revived since the accession of King Juan Carlos, and most of the former Spanish street names have been replaced with Menorquín names.)

On 1st September 1535 the Turkish naval commander Kheir ed-Din Barbarossa ('Redbeard') sailed under false colours into the harbour, determined to exact vengeance for the sack of Tunis by the Emperor Charles V. The Turkish siege threw up a 'Menorcan Benedict Arnold'. His name was Jaime Scala, the town bailiff. He came to an arrangement with Barbarossa to open the town gates, on the condition that he and his friends were spared. The town was sacked, and Barbarossa sailed away with 800 captives. The following year Jaime Scala was put on trial and executed for treason.

In the next century Mahón grew to become the most important town on the island, and the governor Admiral Oquendo moved his residence here. It was during the 18th century that Mahón reached its eminence, when Menorca became part of the British Empire. Today, with a population of some 25,000, Mahón is the capital of the island and its main shopping centre. For refreshment there is no lack of bars, cafés and restaurants, although the same cannot be said of hotels.

Deià. Halfway along, the way bends to the left. Stop here, and look carefully at the building on your left, on the corner — the Teatro Principal. Although it is now used as a cinema, it was originally built as an opera house in 1824 to the design of an Italian architect. If the exterior is pleasant, the interior is exquisite. When the outer door is unlocked, the caretaker will be somewhere about, and she is only too happy to show you inside. I strongly urge you not to miss the opportunity. At the bottom of this steep hill is a pretty little square, the Plaça Reial, at the heart of a pedestrianised shopping area.

Cross over the square and continue in the same direction along S'Arravaleta and into another square, known as the Plaça del Carmé. This is dominated by the massive church opposite you, which was built in 1751 as the conventual church of the Carmelite Order of nuns. It is now known as the Carmen or Carmé church. Baroque in style, its west front is quite plain, although it appears to have once been more ornate. It is worth seeing inside (the side door is in the south wall; you will pass it later in the walk). When digging the foundations for this church, the workmen unearthed many coins and other objects from the Roman period.

Now that the nuns are no longer here, the cloisters and garden of the convent have been put to admirable use as the town's indoor market. Cross to the far side of the square and go up the steps to enter it. This is a convenient place to shop for fruit and vegetables, dairy products, meat and fish. And live snails. Much of the greengrocery will have come from the fertile region of market gardens to the north-west of Mahón known as Es Vergé (Walk 3). Two locally manufactured items of interest are the Mahón cheese and gin. Besides being eaten fresh, the cheese is also used like Parmesan — dried and finely grated. The manufacture of gin was introduced in the 18th century to quench the thirst of the British soldiers and sailors at a time when it was England's most popular drink. There are several varieties, the price varying according to the design of the bottle in which it is sold.

Leave the market by the door diagonally opposite the one you came in by and pass the town's museum. At the end of a short street, you will find yourself in the Plaça de la Miranda. Turn left and walk to the end of the square overlooking the harbour for one of the most beautiful views on the island. Below are the docks, and opposite you is the naval station.

Now retrace your steps and walk back across the square. Carry on to the traffic lights and yet another little square — the Plaça del Príncep. Notice the attractive house on your left, on the corner, No 7. A plaque on the wall awards it a prize for architectural merit. You will see one or two more houses with similar awards. Generally speaking, Mahón does not begin to compare with Ciutadella for the beauty of its buildings, and it looks as though

an attempt was made to
encourage architects to raise
the standard of their designs.

Turn right and walk beside
the Carmen church. (If you
wish to see inside, the door is
on your right.) Walk in front
of the church and cross the
Plaça d'Espanya to the far
right-hand corner, passing
the end of the road leading
down to the port. Turn right,
and cross the Portal de Mar.
Follow the sign 'Ajuntament'

*Pont d'Es Castell*

(town hall) and go up the hill into another square. This is
the Plaça de la Conquesta. Facing you is the statue of
young Alfonso III himself. He was 18 years old at the time
of the Reconquest. The statue was given to the city by the
late General Franco. The young king's generosity in
donating land both to his followers and to the religious
orders of St Francis and St Clare earned for him the title
'the Liberal'. (His successor, Jaime II, thought him far too
liberal, and reclaimed many of his gifts to the orders.)

The building on the left of the square is the church of
St Mary (Santa María), and facing you is the Casa
Mercadel. Once the home of one of Mahón's noble
families, it was built in 1761 on the foundations of the
ancient castle, some of which is incorporated into the
interior. The part of the town you have now entered
contains the oldest buildings still surviving, and stands on
the site of the original town formerly contained within the
medieval walls. The Casa Mercadel is now the Casa de
Cultura. It contains a public library, a picture gallery, and
the town's archives. Turn right in front of the library, and
walk to the end of Carrer d'Alfons III, beneath the arch
shown above. This is known as the Pont d'Es Castell, and
from here you have another enchanting view of the
harbour.

Turn round now, and walk back past the Casa Mercadel and along the narrow cobbled street named after
Alfonso III into yet another square, the Plaça Constitució.
On your right is the town hall, first built in 1613, but
entirely transformed in 1788. This too is open for inspec-
tion. Go up the steps leading from Carrer d'Alfons III to
the entrance beneath the clock in the short wall. The
clock is English, a gift from the first British lieutenant-

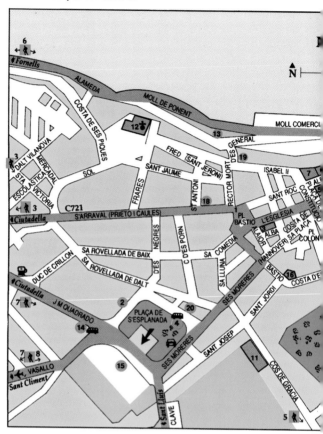

governor, Sir Richard Kane. In the entrance hall are pictures of former governors, the Comte de Lannion and the amiable looking Count of Cifuentes, governor during the period of Spanish rule from 1781 to 1798. There are two inscribed stones of interest. One is the British coat-of-arms that was removed from Fort St Philip when it was destroyed. The other, scarcely decipherable, records the granting of municipal status to the town by the Romans. At the end of Alfons III turn right, walk past the police station and, at the end, turn left along Carrer d'Isabel II. This was the street where the medieval royal palace, and later the British governor's palace, were located. Consequently, the Mahón aristocracy chose to build its homes here. The present houses date from the 18th century and are in a curious mixture of English and Mediterranean styles. The two most apparent debts to English archi-

**MAHON — KEY**

1 Sant Roc Gate
2 Tourist Information
3 Post Office
4 Bus Stops
5 Church of Santa María (St Mary)
6 Casa Mercadel (Casa de Cultura)
7 Town Hall
8 Customs House
9 Market
10 Carmé (Carmen) Church
11 Hospital
12 Church of Sant Francesc (St Francis) and Museum
13 Aquarium
14 Bus Office (TMSA)
15 Monument to the Civil War Dead
16 Teatro Principal
17 Pont d'Es Castell
18 Sala de Cultura (Ermita de Sant Antoni)
19 Military Governor's Headquarters
20 Science Museum
21 Parc Rochina

tecture are the sash windows and the absence of balconies. Sash windows are virtually unknown outside the British Isles, except for here in Mahón. So unused to them were the local swains, accustomed to paying court to the young ladies through their windows, that they nicknamed them 'guillotines' for the risk they now ran.

To appreciate these buildings properly you must look upwards. The main state rooms are on the first floor, the *piso principal*, and many still contain fine furniture made by the first-rate Menorcan craftsmen of the 18th century from the pattern books of English cabinet-makers like Chippendale and Sheraton.

Halfway along the street are the headquarters of the military governor. This is where Alfonso III built his palace in the 13th century, and where the British governor built his in the 18th. At first it was of only one storey, and the style is clearly British colonial. Do not upset the sentry by trying to take a photograph. You may, however, photograph the narrow, arched street beyond it which leads down to the harbour. This is the Costa des General (or Es Pont des General) and was built either by the Moors, or very soon after the Reconquest.

Having investigated the Costa des General, continue along Isabel II. Notice the plaques above numbers 58, 60 and 62, commemorating illustrious inhabitants who were born or lived there. At the end of Isabel II is the Pla des Monestir. Here was the friary of the Order of St Francis (Sant Francesc), and what was the conventual church faces you. It is decorated in a most unusual style, a mixture of baroque and Romanesque. Don't be fooled by the doorway — it was built at the same time as the rest of the baroque façade (sometime in the 17th or 18th centuries). The architect made similar use of primitive features inside. You may find it more difficult to gain admission to this church than the others in Mahón, but if the opportunity presents itself, seize it. Then go through the middle chapel on the right into one of the most exciting ecclesiastical experiences in the town — the Chapel of the Immaculate Conception.

Spanish religious architecture is generally almost puritanically severe — even, as you have already seen, during the baroque era. However, there is one exception. In the 18th century one Spanish architect went overboard in his reaction against this tendency. His name was José Churriguera, and the style which he invented is called after him 'churrigueresque'. Not only did he use baroque decorative invention to excess, he crowned it by doing everything in brilliant white. (Cynics have dubbed the style, not inappropriately, 'wedding-cake architecture'.) The effect, in small doses, can be stunning, as here. Before leaving, notice the *trompe l'oeil* paintings at the top of the pillars beside the sanctuary. Next to the church is the Museum of Menorcan Antiquities.

On leaving the church, first turn left and walk beside it for another view of the harbour, then cross over the square to walk back to the town centre along the Carrer Fred (also called Carrer de Sant Jeroni). Take the first turning on the right, which is Carrer de Sant Antoni. St Anthony Abad ('Abbot') became the patron saint of Menorca, for it was on his feast day, January 17th, that Alfonso defeated the Moors at Es Vergé. Cross over the Carrer de Sant Jaume and, at the end, you come to

S'Arraval (also called Prieto i Caules). On the left, at the corner, is the church *(ermita)* of Sant Antoni, built in classical style. It was restored in 1978 by the Sa Nostra savings bank, and is now the Sala de Cultura, where concerts and exhibitions are held regularly.

Turn left, and there before you is all that remains of the medieval walls, the Sant Roc gate. Pass through the gate, and walk through the middle of the ancient town along the Carrer de Sant Roc. If you like paintings, look out for the art gallery on the right. This road is the start of the C721 which crosses the island to Ciutadella.

At the end of Sant Roc you re-enter the Plaça

*Plaça de S'Esplanada*

Constitució. Facing you is St Mary's Church. It is the main church of Mahón. The present building dates from the middle of the 18th century, but the first church here was begun in 1287, immediately after the Reconquest. Like the Carmen church, its baroque façade is severely plain, but inside it is very different. Two features dominate. One is the magnificent decoration surrounding the main altar, the other is the equally magnificent organ. This splendid instrument was built in Barcelona in 1809 by the Swiss organ builder Kyburz. In the town archives are letters from the bishop to Admiral Lord Collingwood arranging for its transportation and protection at the height of the Napoleonic Wars. It has 4 keyboards, 51 stops and 30,000 pipes. By the south entrance are two tablets which commemorate the French governors of Menorca, Yacinthe-Cajetan, the Compte de Lannion, and the Marquis de Fremeur.

Turn right at the end of Sant Roc (or cross over the square if you have visited the church) and then turn right again into Carrer de l'Esglesia (Church Street), to walk back up another of the ancient streets to the Plaça Bastió beside the Sant Roc gate. Turn left at the end, and walk along a delightful little passage, the Carrer d'Alaior, into Hannover Street. Named after the British royal family at the time Menorca formed part of the Empire, it is one of the principal shopping streets of Mahón. This is quite a steep hill (costa), hence its Menorquín name Costa de Sa Plaça. Turn left and go down the hill, and shortly you pass the square for which the street is named — the Plaça de Colón. Having once more arrived at St Mary's Church, this time turn right along a wide, pedestrianised street, the main shopping street of Mahón — Carrer Nou (New Street).

At the end, turn right in the Plaça Reial, and begin the climb back up Costa d'en Deià and on into Carrer Bastió. At the junction turn left into Ses Moreres and this time walk on the far side of the street. Cross over Carrer Sa Lluna, but when you come to Sa Rovellada de Dalt, turn right. Look carefully for a building on the left with the word 'ATENEO' over the door. This is the science museum and is worth a visit. The intellectual hub of the town, it houses both a library and a natural history museum, as well as providing a meeting-place.

From here, continue along the street and take the first turning on the left which will bring you back to the Esplanade Square where your tour started (**1h30min**).

## 2 SA TORRETA

**Distance**: 11.5km/7.1mi; 3h  **Grade**: moderate

**Equipment**: comfortable footwear, sunhat, raingear, swimwear, picnic, plenty of water, suncream, towel, binoculars

**How to get there and return**: 🚌 or 🚗 to/from Es Grau. By car take the PM710 (Fornells road) from Mahón and in 0.75km turn right along the Es Grau road. Park beside the beach.

**Shorter walk**: Cala Sa Torreta (8.5km/5.3mi; 2h15min; grade, access and equipment as above). Follow the main walk to the 50min-point, then turn right instead of left. Follow the track past one beach, across a headland, past a small cove and on to the beach of Cala Sa Torreta. To return, pick up the main walk at the 1h50min-point.

This walk has just about everything you could ask for. It crosses lovely and isolated countryside. It passes by both the largest habitat for water fowl on the island and one of the least-visited prehistoric *talayot* and *taula* sites, then carries on to a magnificent beach backed by a shaded picnic spot ... that also happens to be adjacent to a breeding ground for bee-eaters. Finally, for the most part it does this along well-surfaced, easily-followed tracks.

**Begin** by walking round the large sandy beach of Es Grau (Picnic 3) to the cliffs at the far side. Climb the path up the cliff and cross the headland. At the top ignore the track which goes off to the right (your return route), and follow the wider track to the left as it curves round the end of a small valley. This track keeps turning to the left, soon entering a wooded area where you will find an open shaded spot just right for a picnic (another setting for Picnic 3; **20min**). In a little while you meet a junction. Ignore the track to the left, and follow the main track as it climbs round to the right. Shortly you will reach the top of your climb and come out of the trees to arrive at another junction. Ignore the path downhill to the left and in 50m/yds go through a gap in a wall. Ahead you will

see Es Grau. Follow the track until the houses have just disappeared from view and you will reach another T-junction. Turn left here, fork left in 20m/yds, and head in the direction of the island known as Illa d'en Colom.

When you reach the cliffs, follow the path down past a little troglodyte house, behind a tiny beach and up the other side. You must now swing to the left, to cut across the headland and reach the coves on the far side. There are several worn paths to choose from, but the easiest on the feet is the one which goes just to the left of an area of low vegetation. Follow the path down to sea level again and round the bay, past two small inlets and one sandy beach, and up the slope on the far side. Follow a tiny sandy path through a gap in a wall and down to the left where it will join a stone cart-track. Mark this junction carefully (the pampas grass should help) because you will need to return along this path at the end of the walk.

Turn left (**50min**) and follow the track southwest. *(But for the Shorter walk, turn right here.)* After 200m/yds go through a wooden gate and pass through two more gates as the track takes you along a pleasant valley before bringing you within sight of the extensive salt-water lagoon of S'Albufera, home to a wide variety of water birds. The track now changes direction (**1h10min**), turning northwest and going through a gap in a wall by a stone shed, before it begins to climb more steeply. Go through another gap and climb up towards trees. After 15 minutes go through a wooden gate and walk between walls for a short stretch. Ignore the track off to the right. Ahead you can see the farm of Sa Torreta. It is your next port of call, but at present you are diverting into a field. On your left the walled-in track is now quite impenetrable, being overgrown with bushes. Unfortunately such tracks are all too common on Menorca, and few of them are as easy to circumvent as this one.

At the end of the track go through a gateway (**1h30min**); you will see some farm buildings a few yards along to your left. Walk towards them and, when you arrive at the farmyard, ignore the gates to the left; go through those straight in front of you. Pass in front of a barn. On your right is the track you will eventually take to continue the main walk; on your left is a modern barn built of concrete blocks. Turn right and follow the narrow path that runs beside this concrete barn across a thistly field to the site of a prehistoric village complete with *talayot* and *taula* in its typical setting of standing stones within an overgrown walled enclosure. It is claimed that the *taula* here is one of the latest, 1000 years separating it from the earliest to be built.

Return to the farmyard and the wide, clearly-defined track, then turn left. Ahead you can see Cala Sa Torreta, your next destination. Pass an old threshing floor, go through a gateway in a wall, and ignore a further gateway on the left. The track descends through wooded country and opens out into a pretty valley, at the end of which you come to the *cala* (17 minutes from the farm). The way turns right to run along the back of a very beautiful and almost always deserted beach. To your right pine trees provide a shaded picnic spot (**1h50min**; photograph below). Beyond the wood, the small holes you may see in the sand bank are the nesting places of bee-eaters. If you are not an ornithologist, look for something the size

*At Cala Sa Torreta pines shade your picnic spot. Nearby is a breeding ground for bee-eaters.*

of a pigeon and as colourful as a parrot.

The track leads you next through trees. Leaving them, it swings left towards the sea and climbs to the right of a small building, running beside a wall to the next cove. Here it moves away from the wall and shortly turns right, away from the sea. In a few minutes it brings you across the headland to another delightful beach. In three or four minutes start to look for the tiny sandy path leading through the pampas grass on the left which takes you back to the Fondeadero de los Llanes (**2h05min**). Go back through the gap in the wall and down to the beach. Round the beach and, at the far side, go through a gap in the rocks just at the water's edge. The path is quite clear now. Follow it as it circles the bay and, beyond the last little inlet, climbs up the cliff. Fork right at the top and cross the headland, this time with the area of vegetation immediately to your left. Once more pass behind the little beach, go through the gap in the wall, and follow the path upwards past the cave house. At the top bear left; ignore two paths on the left, and the track on the right along which you came out. Head downhill towards the sea, with Es Grau clearly visible. At the bottom go straight over the crossing track and up a steepish climb. Ignore the right turn at the top, but follow the track ahead until you regain the beach of Es Grau (**2h45min**).

Do not walk round the beach, but continue in the same direction you have been walking and cross the end of the beach, to a gap between sand dunes. Here take a track which swings to the left through woodland. After six minutes, when you leave the wood, look to your right to see S'Albufera again. The track crosses a footbridge and brings you to a tarmac road. Here turn left and in 300m/yds you will arrive back at the car park/bus stop (**3h**).

*Walk 3 and Picnic 1: The shaded Ermita de Sant Joan, a chapel dedicated to St John the Baptist, offers stone seats and shade for picnicking.*

# 3 ES VERGE AND THE ERMITA DE SANT JOAN

See map on reverse of touring map and photographs pages 39, 44, 56
**Distance:** 8.5km/5.3mi; 2h                    **Grade:** easy
**Equipment:** comfortable footwear, sunhat, raingear, suncream, picnic
**How to get there and return:** As walk 1, page 32
**Very short walk:** Ermita de Sant Joan (4km/2.5mi; 1h10min; grade, equipment, access as above). Follow the main walk to the 40min-point, then skip to the 1h30min point to end this stroll.

T his short and delightful walk is steeped in history. It takes you first along part of the Mahón waterfront and then through the fertile market gardens of Es Vergé, to the little Ermita de Sant Joan. From here you follow Kane's Dyke to its end. Returning to the *ermita*, you make your way back to Mahón along a narrow lane of considerable antiquity, with splendid views over the plain.

**Start out** by standing with your back towards the towering monument to the Civil War dead in the Plaça de S'Esplanada (see town plan on pages 36-37). Leave the square by heading east along Ses Moreres in the right-hand corner. At the end, continue in the same direction, firstly down the Costa de Sa Plaça (Hannover), and then Portal de Mar. This brings you into the Plaça d'Espanya, where you turn right and almost immediately left, to descend steps through Parc Rochina to the harbour.

When you reach the docks, turn left and walk beside the harbour. To your left the cliff looms up, and on top are the remains of the walls of the little medieval town, often incorporated into the 18th-century houses of Carrer Isabel II which now line the edge of the cliff.

On coming to the end of the harbour (**15min**), take the road on the left signposted 'Fornells', not the one which goes across the end of the harbour. This is quite a busy road, and you should walk on the left-hand side of it. However, you will not be on it for long. It is the start of the main road which the first British lieutenant-governor of the island, Sir Richard Kane, had built to link Ciutadella with Mahón in the 18th century (the Menorcans know it as the 'Camí d'en Kane'). It runs parallel with the modern road (C721), about a kilometre to the north, as far as Es Mercadal, from where the C721 follows the line of Kane's road for the rest of the way. Before the British occupation, travel had been along the 'Old Road', the Camí Vell, first built by the Romans. It is significant that whereas the modern road goes to Mahón town, Kane built his road straight to the harbour. That was the only interest Britain had in Menorca — a base for its Mediterranean fleet. Incidentally, Kane arranged for his road to be paid for in a very English way. He put a tax on alcohol.

In 200 metres/yards you come to a junction. Walk a short way straight ahead along the Fornells road, to see the memorial which the Menorcan people raised to Sir Richard Kane in 1924. It is on your right.

Then return to the junction and walk up the hill for 50m/yds, before turning right along a country lane, the Camí de Sant Joan (**30min**). You make your way between some of the most important market gardens on Menorca, which provide Mahón with its salad crops and vegetables. It is very peaceful down here, and the world of the tourist resorts seems far away indeed. It was here, at the head of the harbour, that eighteen year old Alfonso III met and defeated the Moorish army on 17th January 1287 and regained Menorca for Christendom.

In 700m/0.4mi the lane passes a little church on the left, the Ermita de Sant Joan (St John the Baptist; **40min**). This was clearly a place of communal importance in bygone days, with its stone seats around the little square. Now it has a neglected air, but young people at least have not deserted it completely, and it makes a wonderful place for a quiet picnic (Picnic 1; photograph page 44). From here follow the road as it bends to the right. *(But for the Very short walk, skip to the 1h30min-point below.)* After 400m/0.25mi you cross a bridge. The road swings round to the right to join the Fornells road, but your way is along the track which goes off to the left and for some distance runs beside a drainage ditch. Until the 18th century much of this plain was marshland. In order to build his new road across it, Kane had this ditch dug to drain the marsh, transforming it into rich agricultural land. The ditch abounds with vegetation and birds; keep beside it, ignoring all turnings on the right to farmhouses. Eventually you cross a stream, and the gardens give way to orchards. The track narrows into a footpath not long after you have passed beneath overhanging woodland. In the spring the birdsong here reaches the highest decibel level of anywhere on the island.

Where the path divides in a meadow overgrown with brambles and surrounded by field gates, turn round (**1h**). Make your way back to where the track joins the metalled road, and turn right over the bridge, continuing as far as the Ermita de Sant Joan. Turn right (**1h30min**) and walk in front of the church and between the trees. Take the footpath on your left; it climbs up the hill behind a house. I call it a footpath, but from its width and surface you will

*Date palms in Mahón*

quickly realise that it is no such thing. This is an ancient cart-road, which in the days before Kane drained the marsh was the only way from the farms of Es Vergé into Mahón. Where bedrock forms the surface, the deep ruts made by cartwheels over the centuries proclaim how much use this road has seen.

When you come to where the modern road cuts across the ancient one, cross over and, 15m/yds to the left, continue up a sandy path which soon widens to become a stone-paved track once more. Most of the paving is with small uneven cobbles, which was the normal Menorcan way of surfacing roads. Very occasionally, as in one section here (just before the track reaches the outskirts of the town), the paving is much more sophisticated and gives a clue to the origin of the road. Only the Romans surfaced roads with that much care before the 20th century, on Menorca or anywhere else. The old road ends beside an infants' school (**1h45min**). Keep straight ahead on Camí de Dalt de Sant Joan and cross over Carrer Cronista Riudavets. Continue in the same direction along Carrer Santa Victòria, crossing Dalt Vilanova and Santa Escolàstica; then come to a T-junction. Turn right and follow Carrer Sol to its junction with S'Arraval. Now, if you are in a hurry, cross over and follow Sa Rovellada de Dalt; in just over 200m/yds, it will bring you back to the Esplanade Square. Otherwise one more pleasure awaits you, especially if it is early evening. Turn left, and go along S'Arraval as far as the Sant Roc gate. Pass through the gate, go down the hill, cross the Plaça Constitució, and make your way along the narrow cobbled Carrer d'Alfons III between the Ajuntament (town hall) and St Mary's Church. Cross the Plaça de la Conquesta and go on beneath the arch of the Pont d'Es Castell, to gaze out over the Parc Rochina and the harbour. From here, walk back along Alfons III to the Plaça Constitució, turn left and cross the square diagonally, to go up the hill of Costa de Sa Plaça (Hannover) on the far left. Carry on into Ses Moreres and back to the Plaça de S'Esplanada (**2h**).

# 4 FORT ST PHILIP AND MAHON HARBOUR

See map on reverse of touring map; see also drawing on page 18 and photographs on pages 39, 56

**Distance:** 16km/10mi; 4h                             **Grade:** easy

**Equipment:** comfortable footwear, sunhat, raingear, suncream, picnic (or have lunch in one of the restaurants en route), plenty of water, torch (useful for exploring the Marlborough Redoubt)

**How to get there and return:** 🚌 or 🚢 to/from Mahón. By car, park in the car park beneath the Esplanade Square. Alternatively take the ring road round Mahón, following signs for Es Castell. Park at the far side of the town, close to Cala Figuera, and begin the walk at the 25min-point. At the end, turn to the start of the walk and follow the directions for the first 25 minutes to get back to your car.

**Shorter walks:**

1   Mahón and harbour (4.5km/2.8mi; 1h; grade, equipment, access/ return as above; no torch needed). Follow the walk for 28min, then turn left and walk downhill past the petrol depot to the harbour road. Turn left and pick up the walk again, shortly after the 3h15min-point.

2   Countryside and Fort St Philip (12.3km/7.6mi; 3h; grade, equipment as main walk; access: 🚌 to Mahón, then 🚌 to Es Castell, or 🚢 to Es Castell). Pick up the main walk at the 2h55min-point (the military museum in the Plaça de S'Esplanada). Shortly after the 3h15min-point, at Cala Figuera, go up steps by the petrol depot and turn left to climb to the top of the hill. Cross the road, then follow the walk from the 28min-point back to the 2h55min-point. Return by 🚌 from Es Castell to Mahón, then 🚌 from Mahón, or 🚢 from Es Castell.

3   Harbour (4.5km/2.8mi; 1h05min; grade, equipment as main walk; no torch needed; access: 🚌 or 🚢 to Mahón, then 🚌 to Es Castell). Begin the walk at the 2h55min-point (the military museum in the Plaça de S'Esplanada) and follow it to the end.

4   Mahón, countryside and Fort St Philip (11.3km/7mi; 2h55min; grade, equipment as above; access: 🚌 or 🚢 to Mahón). Follow the main walk to the 2h55min-point, where there is a bus stop. Return by 🚌 from Es Castell to Mahón, then 🚌 or 🚢 from Mahón.

This is perhaps the most interesting walk on the island, and the prettiest. The outward part takes you through 18th-century Mahón, on through farming country, and then beside the coast, to bring you to the scant remains of what was once one of the Mediterranean's greatest fortresses: Fort St Philip. You return beside one of its longest and most beautiful harbours.

**Start the walk** in Mahón, referring to the town plan on pages 36-37. Facing away from the monument in the Plaça de S'Esplanada, begin by walking eastwards along Carrer de Ses Moreres in the far right-hand corner. Turn right at the end and walk down the hill of Costa d'en Deià. Continue across the Plaça Reial into S'Arravaleta. Walk along the right-hand side of the Plaça del Carmé into the Plaça del Príncep. Take the right-hand road at the fork ahead, and make your way along the Camí d'Es Castell. The *castell* was the great 16th-century fortress of St Philip, which guarded the entrance to Mahón harbour. After passing the Andrea Doria flats at the end of the town, you will come to a large roundabout (**25min**).

On your left is an arm of the harbour now known as Cala Figuera, overlooked by the town's largest hotel, the Port Mahón. In former times the *cala* was called the 'English Creek', for a freshwater stream ran into the sea here, and ships of the Royal Navy would put in to take on water. Now it is petrol that is stored in the area. *(Shorter walk 1 leaves here.)* Almost opposite the *cala*, at **28min**, a road goes off to the right. *(Shorter walk 2 joins here.)* Follow this road for 50m/yds, looking for a narrow walled-in footpath on the left. Go along the footpath, then up steps to join a wide track, the Camí de Biniatap. Turn left. After a few metres/yards, ignore a track on the left, and follow your track round to the right. In four minutes ignore a tarmac road on the left leading to the houses of Son Vilar. Seven minutes later the Camí de Biniatap acquires an asphalt surface. In one minute ignore another road on the left, and two minutes later cross straight over the road which runs from Trepucó to Es Castell. Continue along a tarmac road past the Es Castell industrial estate.

Some 10m/yds after passing Carrer d'es Fusters on the left the road forks (**50min**): turn right along a rough track between walls. After six minutes ignore a track on the left; seven minutes after that turn right at the next junction. You will see ahead of you a circle of radio masts. In five minutes pass a drive on the right, and soon you will come to the Sant Lluís/Es Castell road. Cross over towards the white farmhouse shown on page 51 and follow the track to the left of it. In three minutes bear right when you reach a tarmac road. As you walk along this road you will have a fine view of the military base of La Mola to your left. In six minutes ignore a lane on your left, and shortly pass the farm of Ses Aubertones. Next door is the military establishment responsible for the aerial masts seen earlier. After you have passed the entrance to the base, turn left on to a wide dirt road signposted 'Horts de Binissaida'. As you do so, look to your right, where between the trees you will see the sturdy tower of a medieval fortified farmhouse (**1h26min**). Follow this road for 600m/0.35mi, ignoring all side tracks, until you arrive in front of large wooden gates set into a very splendid dry-stone wall. Turn left into a narrow walled-in track. Where the new wall finishes, turn right and leave the track by climbing through a gap in the wall. Follow a well-walked path across fields and through more gaps in walls towards the sea, arriving just to the left of a defensive tower built during the Napoleonic War, the Torre d'en Penjat.

Turn left and walk beside the sea (Picnic 2) for 10 minutes, until you reach another, older tower, illustrated on page 18. To the right you can see where stone has been quarried to build the fortifications you are about to encounter. Since everything on the island has been built of stone from time immemorial you will frequently come across old quarries when walking and, near Ciutadella, one that is currently being worked.

Make your way round the tower, and join a tarmac road which turns left to follow the edge of the beautiful Cala de Sant Esteve, known for a hundred years to British servicemen as St Stephen's Creek. Over the creek you can see all that remains of Fort St Philip. After Barbarossa had destroyed Mahón in 1535, the Emperor Charles V gave orders that a fort should be built on the south side of the harbour mouth. The work, entrusted to an Italian engineer named Juan Bautista Calvi, began in 1554. During the 18th century the British spent £1.5 million on strengthening its defences. However, during the Spanish occupation of the island from 1781-98, King Carlos III gave orders for its demolition; a curious act of unilateral disarmament which enabled General Sir Charles Stuart to retake the island without the loss of a single British life when the outbreak of the Napoleonic Wars made a Mediterranean base for the Royal Navy once again imperative.

As you pass a playground on your left you will see a concrete drive leading to a tunnel. This is the entrance to a small fort built to provide crossfire with Fort St Philip. Named after a great British general, it was known as the Marlborough Redoubt. In the final assault in 1781, a captain and 50 men withstood a French force of 700 men. It is said to be connected to Fort St Philip by a subterranean passage beneath the *cala*. When you have explored the Redoubt, continue round the *cala* as it bends to the right. When you have finally walked round the end of it, look carefully for a narrow footpath on your left and climb it. This path is in fact one of the oldest roads on the island, built by the Romans; originally it continued to Mahón.

At the top of the path, stop and turn round before continuing your walk. From here you have a splendid view of the Redoubt. Now bear left and walk to the junction with the PM705 along which once carts trundled and Redcoats marched to the fort. Turn left again, and in four minutes you will come to a crossroads beside a cemetery (**2h17min**). Turn right now along a road signposted 'Sol del Este'. Shortly before the road bends left, climb over a broken wall on your right. Follow the path down to the sea (stepping with care; it is beloved of local dog walkers). This is the setting for Picnic 17, facing more of the few standing remains of Fort St Philip. (You may explore as far as the barbed wire fence, but beyond, as you will see, the *zona militar* is still occupied by the Spanish Regiment of Artillery.) When you reach the water's edge, turn left and walk beside the sea to a gap in a wall (at the right of some houses).

Across the water can be seen the fortifications built on Cape La Mola in the 1840s to replace Fort St Philip in giving protection to the harbour mouth. They were never finished. The large island in front of it is known as Lazareto and was used to house victims of the plague. The high walls, it was hoped, would prevent infection being blown into Mahón.

Carry on, walking between villas and the sea for 10 minutes, rounding the headland and turning into Cala Padera. When you reach the Sol Naciente restaurant, go down steps, cross the tiny beach and walk up a rough track. On joining a tarmac road, Carrer Xaloc, turn right. This takes you into Carrer Gregal. Keep straight ahead at a junction, cross a wide asphalted area, and bear right beyond it into Carrer Lledeig. On your left is the old farmhouse of Santa-Ana which gives its name to the district. Turn right at the junction with Carrer Llevant. You have now entered Es Castell. The name of the town has changed over the centuries. Having grown up as a settlement nestling in the shadow of Fort St Philip, it was first known as Philipstown. When the French attacked the fort in 1756, its houses gave them excellent cover. After

*Farm near the Sant Lluís/
Es Castell road*

the island was returned to Britain, orders were given for Philipstown to be demolished and a new town built further away. It was named Georgetown, in honour of King George III. Like Mahón, its architecture is similar to 18th-century English buildings. When Menorca reverted to Spain, the town was renamed Villa Real de San Carlos, in honour of one of the most enlightened monarchs of the century, Carlos III. Its name was shortened to Villa-Carlos, but is always referred to locally as Es Castell, from its proximity to Es Castell de Sant Felip — Fort St Philip.

Follow Carrer Llevant downhill to the town's larger harbour, Cala Fonts. At the bottom of the hill, turn left into the main street, Carrer Stuart (named after General Stuart). Walk across the Plaça de S'Esplanada — once the parade ground of the British soldiery whose old barracks surround the square. Now one is being turned into housing, while the Cuartel de Cala Corp is the military museum (**2h55min**). *(Shorter walks 2 and 3 begin here; Shorter walk 4 ends here.)* Continuing along Carrer Stuart, you pass the street leading to the smaller harbour, Cala Corb. Carrer Stuart ends at the junction with Carrer Fontanilles. Cross over and bear diagonally right into Carrer Agamenon. Beyond the Hotel Agamenon the road stops: follow a path across a field, beside the harbour. Ahead, the lovely red building is the Hotel del Almirante, named after the admiral Lord Collingwood, commander-in-chief of the Mediterranean fleet, who lived here during the Napoleonic Wars. In seven minutes, when the path divides, keep right, descending to pass in front of some white houses; then take steps down to the harbour road and turn left (**3h15min**).

Follow this road round Cala Figuera. *(Shorter walk 1 rejoins here; Shorter walk 2 climbs up past the petrol depot.)* Continuing beside the harbour, after half an hour you will be at the commercial dock. Climb steps on the left up through Parc Rochina. Turn right at the top, up Carrer Sant Crist, then go left into Carrer Nou. At the end you return to the Plaça Reial. Turn right and climb back up Costa d'en Deià, turning left at the crossroads to follow Ses Moreres back to the Esplanade Square (**4h**).

*Illa del Rei, with Golden Farm (Walk 6) in the background. The large building is the 18th-century British hospital, to which the sick were rowed from ships anchored in the harbour*

# 5 TREPUCO

See town plan of Mahón on pages 36-37 and map on reverse of touring map; see also illustrations opposite, page 56 and cover

**Distance:** 5.3km/3.3mi; 1h15min                    **Grade:** easy

**Equipment:** comfortable shoes of any sort, sunhat, raingear, suncream

**How to get there and return:** as Walk 1, page 32

The prehistoric settlement at Trepucó has a double advantage: it's near to Mahón and has the largest monuments on Menorca. The original excavation of the site was undertaken in 1931 by Dr Margaret Murray and a team from Cambridge University.

Referring to the plan of Mahón, **begin the walk** at the Plaça de S'Esplanada: stand with your back to the tall monument, and leave the square by the far right-hand corner, along Carrer de Ses Moreres. Then take the first turning on the right, Es Cós de Gràcia. In 300m/yds you pass Carrer Ramon i Cajal on the left and, after another 200m/yds, you come to a crossroads, where Carrer de Gràcia comes from the left. Bear slightly right now, to the roundabout. Cross over the dual carriageway and keep straight ahead on a country lane signposted 'Trepucó'. Shortly pass the cemetery on the left. All along this road you will see the *talayot* at Trepucó signposted. Ignore a concrete road on the right, and shortly you will arrive at more crossroads. Turn right to the site (**27min**).

Twice during the 18th century Britain briefly lost control of Menorca to the French — in 1756 (to the Duc de Richelieu) and in 1782 (to the Duc de Crillon, at the head of a joint French and Spanish army). While he was besieging Fort St Philip, the Duc de Crillon mounted his artillery on the *talayot* of Trepucó and built the thick defensive wall which still surrounds the site, using stones from nearby *talayots*. The view from the top of the *talayot* is worth seeing, and although Fort St Philip, on which the French guns were trained, no longer exists, the military base at La Mola on the north of the harbour mouth can be seen, as can Mount Toro in the opposite direction. Yet it is the gigantic *taula* which has pride of place here. The stone circle surrounding it led the first English historian of Menorca, John Armstrong, to conclude (erroneously) that it was the work of Druids. It is the largest on the island. While nearly all scholars now agree on its religious relevance, none is certain what that relevance may be.

When you leave the site, turn left and, on reaching the crossroads, take the road opposite (signposted 'Camí d'en

Verd') and bear right. This pleasant country lane is some 1.3km/0.8mi long and will bring you to the Mahón/Es Castell road at Cala Figuera. En route, in about ten minutes, you will be able to look along the road and across the harbour directly at a lovely red house proudly standing on top of the far cliff. It is Golden

Farm, linked in legend with Admiral Lord Nelson (see Walk 6 and illustrations on pages 52 and the cover).

Just before the end of the Camí d'en Verd look out for an interesting cave on your right (**45min**). The rocks which obstruct the entrance are the result of a partial collapse of the roof, so that it is no longer safe to go in, but do notice the workmanship and thought that has gone into its construction. All manner of receptacles have been carved into the walls, and on the right is a raised area that was possibly where the family slept. Notice especially the way the builder tried to get round the problem of smoke. At the back of the cave are steps going up to a fireplace which he had built at roof level (you can see how the roof is smoke-blackened).

You now have a choice of ways. Either follow the directions below, which take you through the town, or, if you prefer to walk beside the harbour, turn to Walk 4

*The monuments of Trepucó were built during the second millenium BC, at about the time Moses was leading the children of Israel out of Egypt. The first people to see them in modern times believed that only giants could have lifted the huge stones and attributed them to Homer's Cyclops, hence the term 'cyclopean' which is sometimes used as an alternative to 'megalithic' (Greek for 'big stones') to describe this kind of architecture. In this photograph, the taula (the largest on Menorca) rises in front of the massive talayot. In the adjacent field to the west, part of the village has been excavated (see drawing above), revealing amongst much else a 'hypostyle chamber', with typical pillar and one roofing slab still in place.*

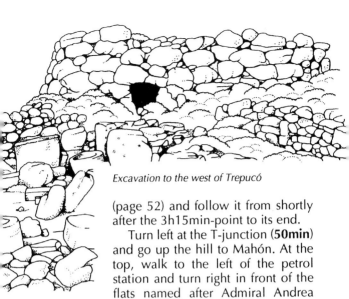

*Excavation to the west of Trepucó*

(page 52) and follow it from shortly after the 3h15min-point to its end.

Turn left at the T-junction (**50min**) and go up the hill to Mahón. At the top, walk to the left of the petrol station and turn right in front of the flats named after Admiral Andrea Doria. Continue along the Camí d'es Castell as far as the second street on the left, Carrer Sant Manuel. Turn left here, and then take the third turning on the right, Carrer de la Infanta. Follow it past three streets on the left. You come to the Carrer de Gràcia. Turn left along it, but in a few metres/yards keep right at the fork, along Carrer Ramon i Cajal. Pass a park on the right. At the next junction (**1h10min**) turn right and follow Cos de Gràcia back to its junction with Carrer de Ses Moreres. Turn left to the Esplanade Square (**1h15min**).

## 6 MESQUIDA BAY

**See town plan on pages 36-37 and map on reverse of touring map; see also cover photograph and illustrations on pages 39, 52**

**Distance:** 16km/10mi; 4h15min

**Grade:** moderate

**Equipment:** comfortable shoes or trainers, sunhat, raingear, suncream, picnic, plenty of water, swimwear

**How to get there and return:** as Walk 1, page 32

It is not easy for those relying on public transport to find their way to the less frequented beaches. Understandably. If buses ran there, they would not be unfrequented for long. Cala Mesquida is an exception. This is surprising, since it is the nearest beach to Mahón. (Consequently it *is* a little busier at the week-end, when people drive out to it.) This walk to Cala Mesquida makes a very enjoyable ramble through attractive countryside, for the most part along metalled roads.

Referring to the Mahón town plan on pages 36-37, **begin the walk** at the bus stop in the Esplanade Square. Stand with your back to the tall obelisk in front of the army barracks. Firstly you must make your way down to the harbour, and the quickest way to do this is to leave the square by the left-hand corner facing you. Cross over Sa Rovellada de Dalt and go down Carrer d'es Negres opposite. Cross over Sa Rovellada de Baix and, when you reach the T-junction with S'Arraval, turn left. Very shortly take the next right along Carrer des Frares. Then take the second turning on the left, Carrer Sol, and follow the road round Sant Francesc Church. Turn right to descend to the harbour along Costa de Ses Piques.

*Looking across the harbour to Mahón, we see the naval station, docks and the city's three great churches.*

Turn left at the bottom and walk beside the harbour along the Paseo de la Alameda. Turn right at the junction and pass by the end of the harbour. Go over a bridge and turn right, to walk up the hill. As you climb the hill, you will pass the central electricity station on your right and, further along, the naval station. You have an excellent view of Mahón from this road, its three great churches being particularly prominent. These are, from right to left as you look at them: St Francis, St Mary and Carmen (see opposite).

As you continue to climb, you will come to a fork in the road. Take the road on the left here, signposted 'La Mola' and 'Cala Mesquida'. La Mola is the peninsula at the harbour mouth. It was there that the Duc de Crillon, commanding a combined French and Spanish army, established his headquarters in 1781 — opposite Fort St Philip on the far shore, where General James Murray and two thousand British soldiers were beleaguered. The following year, King Charles III of Spain ordered the total destruction of Fort St Philip, and thereafter La Mola became the principal fortress guarding the harbour mouth. It is still a prohibited *zona militar* today.

Soon (after **1h10min**) you will pass the entrance to another prohibited military zone on the left, San Isidro. At the very top of the hill, the road to Cala Mesquida goes off to the left. Before taking it, I suggest you follow your present road for 700m/0.4mi, to have a look at Golden Farm. Not that it is 'golden' at all. It is painted that gorgeous red which is so characteristic of the buildings of Menorca. No matter from where you look at this side of the harbour, Golden Farm stands out. From the road you can see the back of the house. You must walk past it, to where the road bends to the right, to see its imposing façade, shown on the cover of the book. From here, too, you have striking views of the harbour and Mahón opposite, as well as of Es Castell to the left.

Menorcans know Golden Farm as 'Sant Antoni', for it was here that a shrine was raised to St Anthony in thanksgiving for King Alfonso's rout of the Moors on his feast day (January 17th) in 1287. But the building's fame derives from its association with Admiral Lord Nelson. In fact the great admiral had little to do with Menorca, far less than he should have done. The naval establishment wanted his squadron here to protect Port Mahón. Nelson differed. His interest lay further east, in Malta, where the people had risen up against the French. When he eventually did sail into Mahón harbour during October 1799, it was with the aim of persuading the governor to send troops to help the Maltese evict the French. He stayed five days, probably here at Golden Farm. Romantically enough, popular legend has it that Lady Hamilton accompanied him.

Retrace your steps now to the road on the right that leads to Cala Mesquida (**1h30min**). This road is quieter than the one you have left, and even more beautiful. Before long you will glimpse Mesquida Bay over on the left. In slightly less than 1km/0.5mi, beyond the junction, leave the tarmac road and turn down a stone track on the left (at the bottom of a hill, near overhead power lines). Closer to the coast, the track becomes sandy. When the houses of Mesquida Bay are quite close, turn down a path on the right, near an electricity pylon. Ahead you will see a 17th-century watchtower. Follow the path past one villa, and turn right just before a second one, walking towards the tower. Next turn left. Pass in front of the house and go down steps, to a concrete path which leads to a road. Turn left on the road and follow it downhill, over a bridge, round and up again. Ignore roads on the right leading to villas and, shortly, you will come to the wide pristine beach of Cala Mesquida (**2h15min**; Picnic 6). It was here that the Duc de Crillon disembarked the bulk of his invasion force on 20th August 1781. The tower on the right is one of many built during the 17th century all round the island, as a deterrent to the many Barbary corsairs who sought refuge in Menorca's secluded *calas*.

You will have to follow the same route back to Mahón, as the prohibited military zone of San Isidro cuts off the best option for a circular walk. As you climb the hill beyond the bridge, look for the concrete path on the right, which will return you to the track. Follow the track back to the asphalt road and turn right. After 1km/ 0.6mi, turn right again, on the Cala Llonga/Mahón road. Walk downhill until you come to the end of the harbour, then turn left, cross the bridge, and turn left again, to walk along the far side of the harbour. Fork right at the junction with Costa de Ses Piques and walk up the hill. At the top, turn right at the T-junction and follow Carrer Sol to its junction with S'Arraval, passing two streets on the right. Cross over and keep to the left along Sa Rovellada de Dalt. Keep straight on at the crossroads and turn right on reaching the corner of the Plaça de S'Esplanada, to arrive back at the bus stops (**4h15min**).

# 7 TORELLO AND TALATI DE DALT

See plan of Mahón on pages 36-37 and map on reverse of touring map; see also photographs on pages 1, 39, 65

**Distance:** 11.3km/7mi; 3h

**Grade:** moderate

**Equipment:** comfortable footwear, sunhat, raingear, suncream, picnic, plenty of water

**How to get there and return:** 🚌 or 🚐 to Mahón; as Walk 1, page 32

**Shorter walk:** Torelló (9km/5.6mi; 2h21min; grade, equipment, access as main walk). Follow the main walk for 1h36min, then turn right and pick up the notes at the 2h15min-point to end the walk.

I t was in 1956 that the name 'Torelló' first appeared on the archaeological map of Menorca, when a very large and magnificent mosaic pavement featuring flowers, birds and animals was discovered. It has since been identified as the floor of an early Christian church. Talatí de Dalt, too, is famed among enthusiasts of Menorcan archaeology as one of the most beautiful of talayotic village sites. This walk also visits two other interesting *talayots,* and so is an excellent way for the visitor to see something of Menorca's prehistoric legacy.

**To begin the walk,** face the lofty monument to the Civil War dead, which dominates the Plaça de S'Esplanada in Mahón, and leave the square by the street in the far right-hand corner, Carrer Vassallo (which is where you will already be if you have come in on the Ciutadella bus). It is the airport road (see plan pages 36-37). Pass the barracks of the Spanish Regiment of Artillery, keep ahead at a large roundabout, then pass a secondary school and sports stadium, before finally reaching the military hospital.

In **12min**, opposite the hospital, turn left along a country lane, the Camí de Baix, signposted to Llumesanas (or Llucmessanes), a village noteworthy for being the only wine-producing region on Menorca. You follow this lane for just over a

*The talayot at Torelló, seen across fields just after the 1h-point in the walk*

kilometre (about three-quarters of a mile). Ignore the turning to the right by No 27.

After an S-bend round a dairy farm, you come to a straight stretch of road. Looking towards your right you can see the fine farmhouse of Sa Cudia, standing behind its imposing palm trees. In a few metres/yards you will come to a narrow, walled-in crossing track (**28min**). Turn right and follow this lane for another kilometre (just over half a mile). Fortunately the dry-stone walls are sufficiently low to afford you a good view of the fields. In them you will see sheds built of loose stones — the way the people of Menorca have been building for three thousand years (see drawing page 109).

At the end of the track (**43min**) you come to a junction with a metalled road. Turn right. In 350m/yds you meet the main road from Mahón to the airport at Sant Climent. Cross this road and carry on towards the industrial estate. Bear slightly left and walk through the estate for 200m/yds. Just before the road bends right, turn left along a track, and in 10m/yds turn left again. Fork left when you are in sight of the farmhouse shown on page 62, Curnia Vey (Curnia Vell on the map), and pass the splendid *talayot* on your left. This is the first megalithic building visitors see on leaving the airport.

After exploring the *talayot* carry on past a quarry and scrapyard, and shortly you will come to a junction with the road which connects the Mahón/Ciutadella highway

*Talatí de Dalt has all the usual features of these pre-historic Menorcan villages — caves, hypostyle chambers, talayot, and taula. In the absence of metals and large trees, the lives of the ancient villagers were dominated by stones. Looking about you, it is apparent how all their building was done with them, but so also was their hunting and fighting (see the note at the foot of page 62). And all this in an idyllic setting (Picnic 5).*

with the airport (**1h**). Opposite are two footpaths. Choose the one on the left. Soon you will enjoy the view shown on page 59. Towards the end it tends to be overgrown, but is passable. Where the footpath joins a lane, turn right and follow the sign directing you to the 'El Sereno' restaurant. Ignore a track on the left in 250m/yds and, in a further 200m/yds, you will arrive at the towering *talayot* of Torelló, unusual in that it possesses an entrance (**1h 17min**). Continue along the track. To your left is the omnipresent Monte Toro. In six minutes turn right along a short track towards a large shed-like structure, sign-posted 'Basílica des Fornàs de Torelló'. It covers the mosaic floor of a church built during the Roman empire. The flowers and animals are African (what a wonderful lion), suggesting that the Menorcan church at this time maintained close links with the church in North Africa, where the great St Augustine was bishop of Hippo.

On returning to the track, turn right and continue in your original direction, soon passing another old quarry on the right and the El Sereno restaurant on your left (open only after 8pm). In 0.5km/0.3mi, at a T-junction (**1h36min**), turn left along another track. *(The Shorter walk turns right here.)* Ignore a turning to the right after 250m/yds and follow the track for 0.7km/0.4mi to a T-junction with a metalled road (**1h50min**). Turn left, and very soon you will see a sign, 'Taula de Talatí'. Cross the wall by the protruding stone steps and walk along the track to Talatí

*Curnia Vey farmhouse*

de Dalt, the prehistoric village shown on pages 1, 60-61 and 65. What a marvellous place it is for a picnic (Picnic 5), with ample shade and enough room to get out of the way of other sightseers.

When you leave the talayotic settlement (**2h**), turn right, and after a few metres/yards turn right again, to return along the same stone track. After just under 1km/0.5mi you arrive at the T-junction (**2h15min**). This time turn left, following signposting for Mahón and Ciutadella. *(The Shorter walk rejoins here.)* Pass under the road connecting the C721 with the airport and, in 150m/yds, keep right at the fork. Carry on along this track, which runs parallel with the C721, for 1km/0.6mi more, and it will bring you to the outskirts of the Mahón industrial estate (**2h36min**). At the end of the track turn left and skirt the estate. On reaching the town proper, bear right at the traffic lights and follow Avinguda Josep María Quadrado back to the Esplanade Square and your bus (**3h**).

The weapon of the Balearic islanders of pre-history was the sling shot. So skilled were they, that they were in great demand as mercenaries for several centuries. When the Carthaginian general Mago sailed into Mahón harbour in 206BC, thereby bequeathing it his name, it was to impress 2000 Menorcan slingers into his army. (It is possible that the very name 'Balearic' comes from the Greek word 'ballein' which means 'to sling'.) Each soldier carried three slings of different sizes, to be used according to the distance, like golf clubs. The stones they used generally weighed about 500g (about a pound), and it was claimed that they were accurate up to 600 paces. Boys were trained from early childhood. Their mothers would place the children's meals up in a tree, and the youngsters had to knock them down with a sling shot. Or go hungry. Their skeletal remains show remarkable development of the shoulder-blade and upper humerus, the latter also being bowed. Having served with the Carthaginian armies, Menorcan slingers later saw service with the Roman legions. Julius Caesar refers to the part they played in his defeat of the Gauls at Alesia in 52BC.

# 8 AN ARCHAEOLOGICAL RAMBLE

See map on reverse of touring map; see also photographs on pages 1, 39, 59, 60-61, 62

**Distance:** 16km/10mi; 4h05min **Grade:** easy

**Equipment:** comfortable footwear, sunhat, raingear, suncream, picnic, plenty of water

**How to get there:** 🚌 to Alaior or 🚐 to Mahón (park beneath the Esplanade Square), then 🚌 to Alaior
*To return:* 🚌 or 🚐 from Mahón

**Shorter walk:** Torralba d'en Salort — Mahón (13km/8mi; 3h20min; grade, equipment as above). Start the walk at the 45min-point, by taking a 🚐 taxi from Alaior to Torralba d'en Salort, thus avoiding walking along the narrow road, which is fairly busy in summer.

S ince this walk takes in two major prehistoric settlements, two additional important *talayots*, two *navetas*, the mosaic floor of a Roman church, and follows what was the main road across the island until Sir Richard Kane built his new highway early in the 18th century, it is clearly a 'must' for the amateur historian and archaeology buff.

**Start** by walking uphill away from the bus stop in Alaior, to a T-junction. Turn left along Carrer d'es Banyer; then after 50m/yds turn right (just before a white wall) along a path. Follow it across waste ground to a road, Sa Carretera. Follow this road to the right for 100m/yds, then cross over and turn left into Carrer Calambusquets (signposted 'Cala En Porter'). Ignore a road on the right to the Coinga cheese factory. Go under the bypass, and follow this busy road for 3km/2mi. In general walk on the left, but make sure you can always be seen by traffic on your side of the road at bends.

After **45min** you will arrive at the prehistoric settlement of Torralba, inhabited for two millennia from 1800BC. Hoskin and Waldron suggest that the *taula* precinct is the most beautiful prehistoric monument in the Balearics, and date it from 890BC. At the foot of the *taula* were found a small stone altar and a bronze bull. From the farm of Torralba Vell, a path leads to the Pou de Na Patarra, a huge well dating from 800BC, with nine flights of steps leading down, and a handrail hewn out of the rock. At the time of writing it is closed to the public and not signposted, but do look to see if it has re-opened.

*Torre d'en Quart (Walk 23). For most of its history Menorca has been subjected to pirate raids, and many old farmhouses incorporate defensive towers.*

Some 20m/yds beyond the site car park, turn left on a track by the side of Torralba d'en Salort farm. *(The Shorter walk begins here.)* Until quite recently the road you followed to Torralba was the continuation of this track, once the main road across Menorca. Proceed through gorgeous farming country for 2km/1.3mi, until you pass on your right the drive to Santa Elisabet (**1h24min**), then Sant Rafel on your left. In three minutes you come to a tarmac road and, when you do, look out for two picturesque old wells — one on your left with a wheel and buckets, and another on your right. Notice too the curious single standing stone inscribed '90 ANYS' (years). Follow the road round to the left. Where you pass beneath power lines there is a road on your right, but ignore that for the moment, because here you make a short detour to the *navetas* of Rafal Rubí.

Turn left and walk 50m/yds to the main road. Cross with care and walk along the road opposite. The *navetas* are well signposted and were built in the talayotic period as burial chambers (**1h41min**). When you leave the *navetas,* walk back along the lane to the main road and cross over. This time take the road on the left when you reach the junction, going under power lines.

Keep going along this road for 1.5km/1mi, until you reach the hamlet of Algendar de Sa Costa, and turn left at the crossroads. In 20 minutes you will come to a sign reading 'Taula de Talatí'. Climb over the wall on your right (use the protruding stone steps) and follow the track to another prehistoric village, Talatí de Dalt (**2h28min**; Picnic 5). Walk 7 will tell you more about the inhabitants of these townships.

Return over the wall and continue in the same direction for a few metres/yards, then turn right along a track (at the right of an aerial mast). If, after a few metres, the path is flooded (and it may well be after rain), divert through the field on your left, leaving it by a gap in the

*Hypostyle chamber, Torre d'en Gaumés (Car tour 2). These buildings are partly underground and roofed with huge stones.*

*Standing stone at Talatí de Dalt*

wall. A little way along this track you come upon a section of very fine paving — a clue to the Roman origins of this road. Of course, linking as it does so many Bronze Age towns, the way itself predates by far the Roman era. Five minutes along the track, look on your right for a narrow path which leads to some caves. Some 200m/yds further on you are directly beneath the airport flight path.

About now ignore a path to the left and, in 200m/yds, turn right at a T-junction (**2h47min**) signposted to a restaurant, 'El Sereno'. You pass this restaurant after 10 minutes (it is only open after 8pm). Soon afterwards, beyond an old quarry, turn left along a short track bearing the sign 'Basílica des Fornàs de Torelló'. This brings you to a Roman mosaic pavement, believed to be the floor of a Christian church. (See notes on page 61.)

Return to the main track and carry on in the same direction for six minutes, when you will reach the *talayot* of Torelló, shown on page 59 (also called 'Torellonet Vell'; (**3h06min**). It is unusual in that it has an entrance leading to a chamber on top. In 200m/yds ignore a track on the right, and in three more minutes emerge on to a road beside the airport landing lights. Turn right, but after 20m/yds turn left on a track. After 10 minutes cross a main road and go along a facing track, pass a scrap-yard and old quarry, and ignore a turning on the right. Now you will see yet another fine *talayot* on your right (**3h27min**). Keep ahead past some large caves. As you approach a T-junction, you have the view of Curnia Vey farmhouse shown on page 62. Turn right at the junction. Follow the track to the right and join a road. Turn right. On your left is the Mahón industrial estate. Walk towards the main road, but turn left just short of it, and follow the quieter road beside the estate into Mahón. Cross the dual carriageway and carry on ahead at the end of the industrial estate (**3h56min**). Having passed the military hospital, sports ground and school, you will come to a roundabout. Keep straight ahead (although you will probably have to make a short detour to cross the road) and follow Carrer Vassallo back to the Esplanade Square (**4h05min**).

# 9 PUIG MENOR AND THE VALLEY OF EJIPTE

**Distance:** 15.5km/9.6mi;4h                                    **Grade:** moderate

**Equipment:** walking boots or comfortable footwear, sunhat, raingear, suncream, picnic, plenty of water

**How to get there and return:** 🚌 to/from the Ermita de Fátima. Leave Mahon along the PM710 road to Fornells, and after 8km you will come to this small church, on the right; park here, beside a football pitch.

**Shorter walks:**

1   Puig Menor (11.8km/7.3mi; 3h; grade, equipment, access as above.) Follow the main walk to the 1h55min-point. At the Binichems crossroads, turn left and retrace your steps downhill. At the bottom turn left to walk beside the stream, then go right along the tarmac road. After some 10 minutes turn left along the track to pass the Sta Magdalena and San Miguel farms. After the cattle barrier turn right and walk past Sa Muntanyeta back to the *ermita*.

2   Binimatzoc and Binichems (10.8km/6.7mi; 2h50min; grade: easy; equipment as above; access by 🚌 to/from Binimatzoc). Drive along the PM710 (Mahón/Fornells) road until, just beyond the KM12 marker, you see a gate on the left signposted 'Binimarzoc', 'Binimarzoch'. Go through the gate and park in the field on the left. Close the gate behind you. Set off along the track where your car is parked, and go through the gateway ahead into woodland. Bear left when you come to a gate on your right, and in 200m/yds go left again. Do the same in a further 100m/yds. After 12 minutes walking turn right at a junction. Turn right at the next junction and pass through a gate, on to a tarmac lane. At the next junction turn left. After 15 minutes you will come to another junction. Here turn left, and in 10 minutes pass the church of Sant Llorens, where the tarmac stops. Carry on for four minutes, to a crossroads. Go straight ahead and follow the main walk from the 1h15min-point to the 3h03min-point, when you will come back to your car.

3   Sa Muntanyeta and the valley of Ejipte (9.8km/6.1mi; 2h30min; grade, equipment, access as main walk). ***Not possible after heavy rain.*** Follow the main walk to the 1h36min-point. Turn left, and follow the track downhill, past the abandoned farm of Ejipte and on across the valley. You will have to climb the final gate, and the last 100m/yds will be quite overgrown and brambly, but passable. A final scramble where the bridge has collapsed will bring you on to the Mahón/Fornells road at the KM10 marker. Turn right and follow the road back to the *ermita*.

4   Binimatzoc and the valley of Ejipte (9.2km/5.8mi; 2h15min; grade, equipment as main walk; access by 🚌 to the Ejipte track). ***Not possible after heavy rain.*** Drive along the PM710 (Mahón/Fornells) road until, just short of the KM10 marker, you see a track on your left, on a bend. Park here. Walk down the track towards a broken bridge and follow a path across the riverbed — and through the brambles beyond it — for two minutes, until you come to a gate that must be climbed. Once on a concrete track, walk across the valley, past buildings and the deserted farmhouse of Ejipte, and climb out the other side. Then follow the main walk from the 1h36min-point, until you pass the KM10 marker on the PM710, when you will be back at your car.

As you sit in the bus on your way to Arenal or Son Parc, the wooded hilly country on your left cries out to be explored. A walk along well-defined tracks and country lanes through this beautiful and fairly isolated part of the island allows you to do just that. The views are often impressive, and there are many shady places for picnics. However, there is one drawback. The last four kilometres (two and a half miles) have to be along a busy main road. If you wish to avoid this, choose Shorter walk 1 or 2.

**Start out** by leaving the Ermita de Fátima (photograph page 68) and turning left along the main road. In 250m/yds turn right over a cattle grid and proceed along a track signposted 'Sa Muntanyeta'. On reaching Sant Carlos farm, go through a wooden gate and pass between buildings; then go on through a gateway. Bear round to the right by the transformer and go through another gate. Follow the track to the next farm, Sa Muntanyeta. Cross a bridge and turn left in front of the farmhouse. Cross the farmyard, to the left of buildings. When you come to a

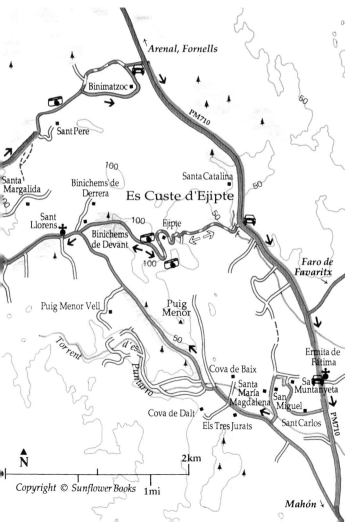

*The Ermita de Fátima, where the walk begins*

field, turn right and follow a farm track round the edge, to a walled-in track. Turn left, crossing a makeshift cattle barrier. In three minutes go through a gate by the farm of San Miguel and keep straight on, passing the entrance to Santa María Magdalena on the right. Follow this track downhill, cross the Torrent d'es Puntarro, and come to a tarmac road (**30min**).

Turn right and in three minutes pass the farm of Els Tres Jurats (The Three Councillors — if you look to the left, at the foot of the hill, you will see them in solemn contemplation). In four minutes you pass between the farms of Upper (de Dalt) and Lower (de Baix) Cova. Shortly after, the tarmac surface ends at a junction, where you turn left and walk beside a stream on your right.

After 100m/yds turn right. In a further 100m/yds, ignore the track on the left and carry on straight ahead. Now the long climb begins. The track ascends steadily and gently to rise 80m/265ft over the next 2km/1.3mi, through dense bushes and attractive scenery. The hill on your right is Puig Menor ('Smaller Peak'), which has given its name to this district. In 20 minutes the ascent briefly levels out and you pass a track on the left, which leads to the farm of Puig Menor Vell. Some nine minutes later you will see ahead the little church of St Lawrence (Sant Llorens).

After a final climb you reach Binichems de Devant (**1h15min**). Turn right at the junction. *(Shorter walk 2 comes in here, and keeps straight ahead.)* Go through the red iron gates, into a field. (Do not follow the track which leads between the farm buildings to Binichems de Derrera.) Walk ahead now, with the farm buildings on your left. Go through a gateway and enter a pine wood. Shortly, go through a gap in a wall. Then the track swings to the right. You can find shady picnic sites

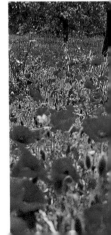

virtually anywhere now. Beyond a further gap, the track begins to descend, and if, after climbing an iron gate, you go forward a few metres, as you gaze over the valley of Ejipte you will enjoy some of the best views on the island (**1h36min**). Puig Menor stands out to the right with its triangulation marker. Ignore the downhill track to the left. *(Shorter walk 3 descends this track; Shorter walk 4 climbs it and joins the main walk here.)* Carry on to the right for a few more metres/yards, you will discover a fine place to enjoy both your picnic and another view.

Turn round now and follow the track back to Binichems de Devant (**1h55min**). Ignore the track on the left that you ascended. *(But for Shorter walk 1, turn left downhill here.)* Keep straight ahead and pass the little church of Sant Llorens. On tarmac now, walk forward for 10 minutes, then turn right. Over to your left there is a quarry being worked. Follow this road for 15 minutes, until you arrive at a Y-junction, where you turn right. After eight minutes the tarmac ends and you go through a gate onto a track, shortly keeping left at a fork, and not long after that going through another gate. Nine minutes later turn right at the next fork. After eight minutes you will reach Binimatzoc farm (**2h52min**). Ignoring a walled-in track to the left, go round the field edge, up to the farmhouse and left across the farmyard.

Follow the track round the next field edge until you come to a gate opening on to the Mahón/Fornells road (**3h03min**). *(Shorter walk 2 ends here.)* Turn right. Now you have an hour's walk downhill back to your car at the Ermita de Fátima. The scenery is pleasant enough; the traffic is the drawback, but there is no way of avoiding it. Keep to the left in general, but make sure that you can always be seen by traffic on your side of the road at bends (**4h**).

# 10 MONTE TORO

**Distance:** 13.8km/8.6mi; 3h35min       **Grade:** strenuous

**Equipment:** comfortable footwear, sunhat, raingear, suncream, picnic, plenty of water

**How to get there and return:** 🚌 to Alaior or 🚌 to Es Mercadal (park in the town centre), then 🚌 to Alaior
*To return:* 🚌 or 🚌 from Es Mercadal

**Shorter walk:** Es Mercadal — Monte Toro — Es Mercadal (7km/4.3mi; 2h20min; grade, equipment as above; access: 🚌 or 🚌 to Es Mercadal). From Es Mercadal join the main Mahón/Ciutadella road (C721) by whichever street you please, and turn left in the direction of Mahón. Once out of the town, turn left along the first road you come to: the Camí d'en Kane, or 'Kane's Road'. Follow the road uphill for 1km/0.6mi (about 20 minutes) and then join the main walk at the 1h53min-point.

Every visitor to the island will wish to ascend to the summit of Monte Toro, Menorca's loftiest hill (at only 358m/1175ft it just merits its name 'mountain'). The easiest way is to drive up, which most people do. For the energetic and those without cars, this walk provides an enjoyable alternative, uniting an interesting country walk with an easier climb (at least to the 200m contour), than the road from Es Mercadal offers.

The town of Alaior is the third largest on Menorca. It was founded not long after the Reconquest in 1304 by King James II of Mallorca, on the site where previously the farmhouse of Ihalor had stood. Some guide books claim that it is the prettiest town on the island. There are two buildings of special interest. One is the parish church of Santa Eulalia, fortified by the townspeople in 1558 after both Mahón and Ciutadella had been sacked by Turkish pirates. The other is the 17th-century Franciscan convent passed at the start of the walk. Alaior is best

*Ever since Sir Richard Kane introduced British breeds of cattle, dairy farming has been an important agricultural activity on Menorca.*

*The 17th-century sanctuary on the summit of Monte Toro, where there is also an old defence tower and a memorial to the men killed in the African War.*

known for its ice cream, but shoes and cheese are made here too.

The bus stop in Alaior is in Carrer Sant Joan Baptista de la Salle, in front of a large sports complex. **Begin** by walking southwest away from the bus stop and turning right along the street running along the left-hand side of the sports complex, Carrer Mestre Duran. They began to construct the large building which you see in front of you in 1624. Originally it was a Franciscan convent. Its pink church was dedicated to San Diego (one of the many aliases of St James, which itself is an alias — since his real name was Jacob). The local populace refer to it as Sa Lluna, and it has now been converted to housing. Turn left in front of it along Carrer Les Escoles, then turn right and pass its entrance — though not without turning in to look at the picturesque cloister, said to be reminiscent of the Spanish missions in California.

Turn right and follow Carrer Sant Diego along its west wall, forking right at the end to go downhill along Carrer d'es Regaló. Turn left at the end, then fork right up Carrer Costa d'es Pou. At the top of the hill you come to a junction, and turn right along Carrer d'es Porrassar Vell. Continue to the right of a palm tree, and then along the side of a tiny square, the Plaça Espanya, at the end of which you turn right into Carrer Camí Nou (formerly San Pedro). Look out for the street on your right dedicated to Sant Pancraç (patron saint of British Rail?). Pass a small garden with a playground and the church beside it, and you have now crossed Alaior (**16min**).

Turn left along a track at the back of the church. Ignore the first track to the left in 10m/yds, but in five minutes turn along the second one. Ahead you can see your destination. In ten minutes ignore a track to the left, and carry on ahead by Estancia d'en Agusti. Seven minutes later again keep straight ahead when an obviously more used track goes once more to the left. The track that you are on is the continuation of the one followed by Walk 8

71

— the main road linking the towns before Kane's road was built. After going under power lines you begin to walk through woodland. At **55min** you go under the power lines for a second time and pass the entrance to Estancia de Sant Josep farm. Eight minutes later ignore another track on the right. Five minutes later, just after crossing a stream, you come to a T-junction: turn right (**1h08min**).

Some 14 minutes after the T-junction you meet another junction, this time with a metalled road. This is the Camí d'en Kane which from here to Es Mercadal follows the same line as the older road. Turn left and follow it for half an hour, passing three large farms en route: S'Astansia, Bini Llobet and S'Aranjassa. After the last of these the road goes downhill and bends to the left. Ignore a track to the right on the bend which leads to the farm of Sant Joan de la Creu, but within 50m/yds turn right through a gate (**1h53min**). *(The Shorter walk joins here.)* Climb a track past the drive to Sant Carlos farm and in 12 minutes turn right towards that of Rafal d'es Frares. Go through a gate, and follow the track round to the left in front of a farm building; then keep left again, to pass to the left of the farmhouse. Go through a gateway and walk up the side of a little valley, until you go over a cattle grid and join the tarmac road from Es Mercadal (**2h16min**).

Turn right and in 200m/yds pass the KM2 marker. The road winds up Monte Toro. It is wide enough for you to keep out of the way of traffic, and occasionally you may be able to take a short cut. It will take you about 45 minutes to climb to the summit. The 17th-century convent buildings, shown on page 71, house a cafeteria and toilets, as well as a gift shop. Outside, the statue of Christ gazes a little forlornly, I fancy, at the emblems of the more recent gods of the 20th century (**2h50min**).

Your descent is very much quicker! Keep on the road this time, and you should be at the roundabout at the foot of the hill in 40 minutes. Go straight over the roundabout and enter Es Mercadal. Pass to the right of a school, then cross diagonally the car park beyond it, to the sign that reads 'Bus'. Follow the sign to the bus stop in Avinguda Metge Camps (**3h35min**).

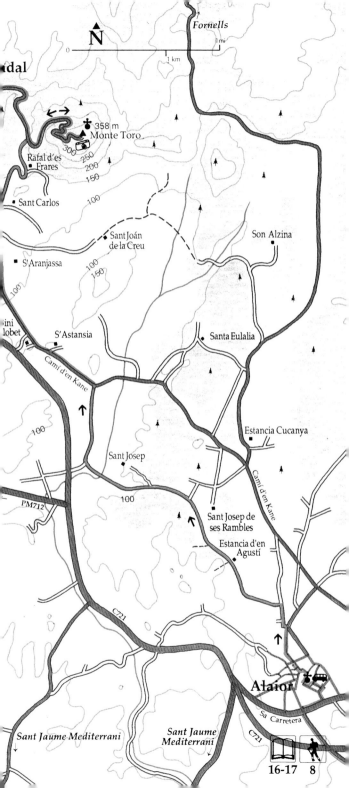

## 11 SON BOU, SANT TOMAS AND BINIGAUS

See also photograph page 4

**Distance:** 14.3km/8.9mi; 4h10min          **Grade:** moderate

**Equipment:** comfortable footwear, sunhat, raingear, swimwear, towel, suncream, picnic (or have lunch at one of the restaurants en route), plenty of water, binoculars

**How to get there and return:** 🚗 to Son Bou (park behind the beach) or 🚌 to Son Bou or Club San Jaime at Sant Jaume Mediterrani. From the bus stop in Son Bou, walk down the road to the beach and turn left; from the Club San Jaime bus stop follow the path behind the bus stop across the marsh to the car park. Go on to the beach and turn left. *Note:* Those of you staying at Sant Tomàs can join the walk wherever is convenient after the 1h09min-point. When you reach Son Bou, turn to the start of the walk, and follow it back to Sant Tomàs.

**Shorter walk:** Son Bou beach and the marshes (9km/5.6mi; 2h30min; grade, equipment, access as above.) Follow the main walk to the 1h09min-point. Turn right instead of left, and continue the walk from the 2h49min-point to the end.

Most of the beaches of Menorca are to be found either around large bays or at the ends of small *calas*. With one exception. Beginning at Son Bou, there is a beach which, save for a couple of 'blips', extends northwest in a straight line for some six kilometres (3.75 miles). This walk is designed to allow you to enjoy its shore, and for variety brings you back across the ends of two valleys dense with vegetation and beside a marsh, all teeming with bird life. Beyond the 1h09min-point the walk is linear, so that you can turn round whenever you choose.

**We begin** by turning *left* along Son Bou beach and walking to the very end — for two reasons. One is that the cliffs here contain one of the earliest housing developments on the island, a large number of cave dwellings dating from the first days of human occupancy of the island (see page 11). The other is to see the remains of an ancient Christian church built during the Roman Empire, with a baptismal font carved out of a single stone in the shape of a four-leaf clover.

From the church turn about and walk to the other end of the beach. I always paddle (hence the slow time for

this section), but some of you may prefer to explore the dunes and look over the marsh, famous for the variety of birds that inhabit it. At the end of the beach, the Punta Radona has a slight elevation where you can look over the countryside (**53min**). Carry on in the same direction for 13 minutes, now along low cliffs; then follow the path inland beside a pine wood to a junction (**1h09min**).

Turn left. *(The Shorter walk turns right here.)* Follow the path beside the wood until you come to the grounds of the Hotel Victoria Playa. Turn left, walk through the wood, then turn right and cross over a subterranean building, on to the beach of Sant Tomàs. Either continue along the beach or, should you wish to explore Sant Tomàs, turn right and walk along the main street, until you come out of the resort at the end of the Es Mercadal/Sant Tomàs road by a restaurant and bar (**1h42min**).

Beyond is the beach of Binigaus. Again you have the choice of walking along the beach, or on a path which runs beside a wall at the back of the dunes. After 10 minutes you reach the end of the Barranco de Binigaus (**1h52min**). On the sand now, continue until the beach finally ends at the foot of cliffs; then turn round to retrace your steps until you have left the beach in Sant Tomàs by the Hotel Victoria Playa.

Turn left through the wood beside the hotel grounds, and right on leaving the wood. At the end of the wood (**2h49min**) the path you followed earlier comes in from the right. *(The Shorter walk rejoins here.)* Carry on straight ahead for 100m/yds. Then turn left round the corner of the field and make for the trees ahead. The path brings you to a good wide track where you turn right. In seven minutes you reach Atálitx farm. Go through a gate, cross the yard, and continue along the walled-in track opposite (**3h01min**). In four minutes ignore the track on your right leading towards the sea, and go through the gate in front of you. The track now bends inland beside the Torrente de Son Bute, bringing you in a further four minutes to a

*Troglodyte home (3h17min) and the marsh at Sant Jaume, from where you make your way between tall reeds back to Son Bou.*

gate, almost certainly padlocked. Climb the wall by the fig tree. In eight minutes you will come to an ancient troglodyte home on your left, sometimes now used as stabling (**3h17min**; photograph above), and a gate on your right. (The more energetic among you may wish to continue along the valley straight ahead. When the track ends, return to this point.) Turn right through the gate and cross the valley on the causeway. On the far side, at a junction (**3h20min**), turn right. (Once again, you may wish to explore the track to the left. Return to this point and keep ahead.)

In six minutes pass Son Benet farm, where the photograph on page 4 was taken, and shortly go through a gate, ignoring a track on the left. In four minutes pass a very old farmstead, Ses Canassies. The name, given to it by the Moors, means 'The Christian Church', and was inexplicable until 1951, when the 5th-century basilica you saw at the start of the walk was excavated.

In seven minutes the track bends right in the direction of Sant Jaume which you can see ahead. Ignore a track through a field on your left, and follow another causeway over the Barranco d'es Bec. At the far side an iron gate gives on to the car park of the Aparthotel Las Marismas (**3h40min**). Turn right at the entrance to the car park and follow the street down towards the sea. Turn left and walk beside the marsh the length of Sant Jaume. In 22 minutes you will arrive at the Club San Jaime bus stop, in front of the shopping centre. Unless you are ending the walk here, now follow the footpath behind the bus stop. It takes you through the marsh shown above. You will emerge at the Son Bou car park. Turn left and walk away from the sea, eventually up the road. The Son Bou bus stop is on your right, just back from the road (**4h10min**).

# 12 THROUGH THE DEEP SOUTH

**See also photograph page 26**

**Distance:** 12km/7.5mi; 3h                    **Grade:** easy

**Equipment:** comfortable footwear, sunhat, raingear, swimwear, towel, suncream, picnic (or lunch at a restaurant en route), plenty of water

**How to get there:** 🚌 to Sant Lluís or 🚐 to Punta Prima, then 🚌 to Sant Lluís.

*To return:* 🚌 or 🚐 from Punta Prima

### Shorter walks

1  S'Algar — Punta Prima (4.5km/2.8mi; 1h10min; grade, equipment, return as main walk; access: 🚌 to S'Algar). From the bus stop, walk down to the sea-front, turn right and follow the main walk from the 1h58min-point to the end.

2  Trebalúger and Rafalet (8km/5mi; 2h; grade, equipment as main walk; access: 🚌 or 🚐 to Sant Lluís; return: 🚌 from S'Algar). Follow the main walk for 1h58min, then turn right and walk uphill to the bus stop in the centre of S'Algar; alight in Sant Lluís if you left your car there.

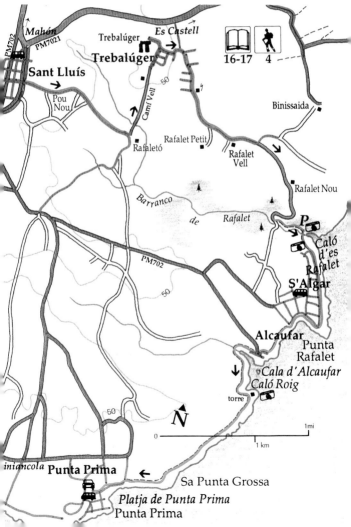

This is a walk of contrasting scenery. At first meandering through farming country, it later follows the coastline, visiting the delightful holiday resorts of S'Algar, Alcaufar and Punta Prima. The town of Sant Lluís was built by the French during their seven-year occupation of Menorca from 1756 to 1763. The king of France being Louis XV, the church here was dedicated by the French (Galli) to St Louis (Divo Ludovico) in 1760, as the inscription across the front proudly proclaims. Hence the name of the town. The interior of the church, though simple, is worth a visit before you start your walk. Also of interest is the windmill in the centre of town, near the bus stop, which has been converted into a museum.

**The walk begins** in the little square, the Plaça Nova, beside the bus stop in the town centre. Standing with your back to the square and facing the windmill, turn left and walk away from it southwards along Carrer de Sant Lluís. Turn down the second street on the left, Carrer de Sant Antoni, and follow it to the dual carriageway. Cross over and continue straight ahead in the direction of Pou Nou. Ignoring several tracks to the right signposted 'Es Pou Nou', follow the country lane for a quarter of an hour. On your left you will see the imposing *talayot* of Trebalúger which is to be your first port of call. When you come to a T-junction before the farm of Rafaletó, turn left along a walled-in track, the Camí Vell (**23min**).

After 10 minutes you will arrive at the village of Trebalúger, where the Camí Vell becomes metalled. Two minutes later turn briefly right at a T-junction in front of

a house, then almost immediately left, to continue in the same direction as before, ignoring streets to the right. In three minutes turn left into Camí d'es Talaiot by the sign 'Talaiot de Trebalúger' to come to that fine cyclopean building you saw earlier (**41min**). Unlike most *talayots* today, this one has steps leading up to an entrance, beyond which is a walled enclosure.

On leaving the *talayot*, retrace your steps to the Camí Vell and turn right. When you come to a T-junction, turn left into Carrer de Sa Torre. Ignore two streets on the right, before turning right into Camí de Rafalet. Stay on this road as it winds through the village. You will pass many side streets; ignore them. Fifteen minutes after leaving the *talayot* you will walk out of the village, passing power lines and a transformer on your left. After three minutes ignore a track on the right leading to the farm of Rafalet Petit but, three minutes later (just before you come to a farm building), look left: in the distance you will see a circle of military aerial masts and, between the trees, the tower of a medieval fortified farmhouse at Binissaida. Ignore another track to the right on a bend. In three minutes the lane bends left, but straight ahead there is a gate between white pillars, and a track (**1h08min**). Go through (or, more probably, over) this gate and follow the track past the lovely farmhouse of Rafalet Nou, beyond which you will catch sight of S'Algar.

Soon the track enters woodland. In four minutes go through a gateway and then downhill to the left. Two minutes later go through a gate on your left, signposted

'Barranco de Rafalet' (**1h24min**). The path takes you through a wood of mainly holly oaks for six minutes. At the end of the path is the delightful setting for Picnic 14. On your right, in the corner, is a tiny path up which you will eventually continue your walk. But not before you have pressed forward to discover the minuscule Caló d'es Rafalet.

*Looking ahead to the tower on the headland at Alcaufar (shown in close-up on page 26), from the promenade at S'Algar. Here, off southeast Menorca, the ill-fated English Admiral Byng fled from the French fleet, so losing the island to the French in 1765 … and his life to a firing squad a year later.*

Return to the path and, after a short scramble, bear left at the top of the cliff. Follow one of the paths beside the creek to the end. All paths lead ultimately to the apex of the field, where a stile *(botador)* takes you over a wall to the road. Turn left and walk down the road beside the sea. At the bottom of the hill, where the road bends right, keep ahead on gravel to the sea, then turn right along the promenade. At **1h58min**, at the end of the promenade (where the photograph on pages 78-79 was taken), keep left and walk between S'Algar Diving Centre and the sea. *(Shorter walk 1 joins here; Shorter walk 2 turns right.)* Continue between the sea on your left and a swimming pool/restaurant on your right, towards a line of small white posts (**2h**). Go through a gap and turn right. When you come to a wall, turn left and follow a well-walked path along the coast for five minutes, to a metalled road. Turn right; it is signposted 'Playa/Beach'. The road bends left to a T-junction, where you turn right. Follow this street and make your way down to the beach of Alcaufar.

Cross the beach and go through a gate on the far side. Follow a path to the left and uphill; ignore the ones which descend to the water's edge. The path will lead you round a headland, past the tiny Caló Roig, and after 16 minutes up to the watchtower shown on page 26 (**2h30min**). On leaving the watchtower, follow the path southwest along the coast for half an hour. To your left is the Illa de l'Aire.

It was in May 1756 in these waters that Admiral John Byng had his ill-fated encounter with the French fleet. The British garrison in Fort St Philip had been besieged for two months by a French army commanded by the Duc de Richelieu that had come ashore at Ciutadella. Eighty-two year old General Blakeney waited for the Royal Navy to relieve his men. At last the garrison saw the fleet arrive. Out sailed the Marquis de Galissonière to engage it, but soon withdrew into Mahón harbour. Then, to the horror of the defenders, the British fleet turned about and sailed back to Gibraltar. Blakeney surrendered, and for seven years Britain was without a Mediterranean naval base. Byng was recalled and court-martialled at Portsmouth. Found guilty of negligence, he was executed by firing squad on board a captured French vessel, the Monarque, on 14th March the following year, 'pour encourager les autres,' as Voltaire wryly observed in *Candide*.

On reaching Punta Prima, follow the road to a left-hand bend at the end of the beach. Cross over and walk along Carrer de Xaloc (by the Hotel Xaloc) to the bus stop (**3h**).

# 13 CALA CALDERER
## AND THE CANAL DE SANT JORDI

**Distance:** 12.3km/7.6mi; 3h      **Grade:** moderate

**Equipment:** walking boots or comfortable shoes or trainers, sunhat, raingear, suncream, picnic, plenty of water, swimwear, long trousers

**How to get there and return:** ⊕ only. Take the main C721 Mahón/ Ciutadella highway to Es Mercadal. Coming from Ferreries, enter the town by the first street on the left, and from Alaior by the last street on the right (beyond the windmill). After 50m/yds bear left for 'Playas Costa Norte' and leave the town along a narrow country road. Ignore the first road on the right, but after 6.5km turn sharply right for Binimel-là. After 0.5km turn left into a wide dirt road and park at the side.

M ost of the walks on Menorca are over fairly flat terrain. This walk is an exception, being distinctly undulating. It takes you through one of the most isolated parts of the island, overlooking the Canal de Sant Jordi. It also passes Cala Calderer on the north coast, a deserted beach which is unfortunately strewn with flotsam. From start to finish the way is along well-defined tracks.

**To start out,** leave your car and return to the tarmac road. Turn right in the direction you have just come. When in 0.5km/0.3mi you reach the junction, turn right again in front of the gate to Bini Alás and cross a bridge. In two minutes turn right between cream-coloured gate-

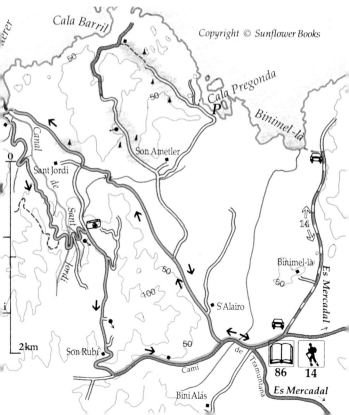

posts. Climb steadily along a track towards the farm of S'Alairo, which you will pass on your right after five minutes. After eight minutes keep straight ahead, ignoring the entrance to Son Ametler on your right (**25min**). Gently descend and, after 15 minutes, climb over the wall beside a red iron gate.

From here the track crosses open fields, going over a stone bridge in four minutes and through a gateway. Go through another gateway and after 200m/yds turn right, pass beneath power lines, and go through a gap in a wall. In a minute go through a gateway and follow the track as it winds through pine trees. In four minutes go through another gap, leave the wood and cross an open field. There is a little dwelling ahead. After another gate, the track runs beside a low wall to the left and, in seven minutes, you arrive at the beach of Cala Calderer (**1h 05min**). This is a good place to relax and picnic, although there is no shade but plenty of debris!

When you move on, walk across the beach. Do *not* go through the wooden gate *or* take the track past a small building, but turn left to pass an unfinished breeze-block house, which often has a herd of Friesian cattle (or even a bull) as squatters. From here take a wide track across a culvert over the end of a valley, then swing right to climb up the side of the valley. At the head of the valley, follow the track round to the left and up through a gateway. At the top turn left and start to descend, before sweeping round to the right and beginning the descent into the next valley. On a hill to your left, on the far side of the Canal de Sant Jordi, is the farm which gives the valley its name, and around which your walk will circle for the next three-quarters of an hour.

Pass through a gateway in a wall and, at the bottom of the valley, go over a concrete bridge and through a gateway. Turn left after the bridge and climb up the far side of the valley, turning right at the end. Up ahead and to the left you can see a gateway in the wall. Follow the now slightly indistinct track up to that gateway, where it becomes more distinct. In two minutes you pass through another gateway. In four minutes the track bends to the right to round another valley, a process that is to be repeated several more times. Go through a wooden gate and follow the track to the left, shortly to swing down to the right to cross another valley. At the end of the valley, as you turn left, ignore an overgrown track coming down on your right and, in a few minutes, repeat the exercise round another valley, the Canal de Sant Jordi itself.

Having completed your circuit of that valley, you come to a junction, some 40 minutes from the beach (**1h50min**). Turn left downhill. In three minutes pass a well and cistern on the right, as you make your way round yet another valley. Five minutes beyond the cistern, a final hairpin bend brings you to a gate set in a wall and to a lovely view ahead — Binimel-là (setting for Picnic 12) and the lighthouse at Cape Cavallería beyond it (**2h**).

Do not go through the gate on the left, but turn right and follow the track beside a deep valley on the left, with fine views. In three minutes you reach another junction. Ignore the track downhill on the left; your way is to the right and upwards. In 12 minutes go through a gate and in six minutes pass by two gates leading into fields on your right. Ignore the track opposite them which leads to another cistern. Go through a gateway and pass to the left of a low stone wall. After passing a stone hut on the left, go through another gateway: in front of you now is the farm of Son Rubí. Here the track forks. Go right, straight down to a gate. From there you follow the track to the left of the house, passing between it and the outbuildings, finally turning to the right. Go through a gate, and follow the track downhill for six minutes, until a red iron gate gives you access to a metalled road (**2h32min**).

Turn left and in 10 minutes pass a deserted cottage on your left. Ten minutes beyond it, you should be back at the bridge, having passed the entrance to S'Alairo. At the junction opposite Bini Alás turn left and, in 0.5km/0.3mi you will arrive back at the Binimel-là turning and your car (**3h**), within easy reach of Picnic 12 (see page 18).

## 14 AN UPLAND WALK

**Distance:** 17km/10.5mi; 4h05min        **Grade:** strenuous

**Equipment:** walking boots (preferably, or comfortable footwear), sun-hat, raingear, suncream, picnic, plenty of water

**How to get there and return:** 🚌 or 🚐 to/from Ferreries. Park beside the C721 where convenient *(but see Shorter walk below).*

**Shorter walk *(recommended for motorists):*** Eliminate the steep climb at the beginning of the main walk (10.5km/6.5mi; 2h40min; grade, equipment as above; access by 🚐 only). By car, approach Ferreries from Es Mercadal on the C721. Some 200m/yds short of the KM28 marker, turn right along a road signposted 'Camí Ruma — Sant Patrici' and follow it for 2.8km, to the top of a steep hill. Drive a short way past Sant Francesc farm to avoid the bend, and park where convenient, taking care not to block any access. Walk back round the farm buildings towards the hill and turn left. Follow the main walk from the 47min-point to the 3h25min-point, when you will have returned to your car.

**Longer walk:** Extend the main walk with a visit to Binimel-là beach (22km/13.7mi; 5h15min; grade, access/return, equipment as main walk, but take swimwear and a towel as well). Follow the main walk for 2h02min, then turn sharp right in the direction of Binimel-là (see map page 81). After 0.5km/0.3mi, turn left along a wide dirt road. After 1km/0.6mi, you will pass through a gateway and enter the property of Binimel-là. In a further 1km/0.6mi the track forks: you can clearly see the beach that the track to the left would take you to (and the start of Picnic 12) but, if you carry on straight ahead, you will also come to a pleasant, smaller beach. Take your choice. From the beach retrace your steps to the end of the dirt road and turn right. At the junction in 0.5km/0.3mi, keep straight ahead towards a bridge, and follow the main walk from the 2h02min-point to the end.

The landscape of Menorca is one of gentle green hills. There are no real mountains on the island. This walk is the nearest one comes to a mountain walk: it circles a quite deep gorge, and the initial ascent is fairly steep. For the most part you will be on good tracks or asphalt country lanes. There are splendid views from the top, and

*Cattle shed — typical of the many encountered on this walk*

it is unlikely that you will meet another living soul. I am always surprised on these walks by the feeling of total isolation you can experience on such a small island.

**Start** by walking out of Ferreries on the C721 towards Es Mercadal. After 400m/yds you reach a lane on the left signposted 'Camí Ruma — Sant Patrici'. Turn along this lane (**10min**). In 11 minutes go past a farm and ignore the track on your right. In another two minutes pass on your left an imposing yellow farmhouse, splendidly proclaimed as 'Nura Ramadería Diplomada — Hort Sant Patrici'. As you ascend along this road, the allotments which border it will hold your attention. Some **28min** into the walk the road forks. The road on the left is signposted 'Camí de Marcona', but your way is to the right. In seven minutes the tarmac is replaced by concrete as the gradient stiffens. No doubt you will feel the need to pause and admire the scenery from time to time. As you do so, notice the aerial installations of the military base at Inclusa on Monte Sa Torre, part of the American worldwide military communications system. Your immediate goal is the farm of Sant Francesc on the top of the hill, reached in **47min**. *(The Shorter walk begins here.)*

Turn right here along a stone track — observing the pictures of St Francis of Assisi on the wall as you do so. The way is thankfully level now, as the track takes you eastwards. In seven minutes, go over a cattle grid, and you will find an admirable field in which to picnic, with open spaces, vistas, and shade. And goldfinches. I once saw here the biggest flocks of goldfinches I have seen anywhere. The track continues with lovely views of the surrounding hills and, over the valley to the left, the distant beach of Binimel-là and the sea. Go over another cattle grid and, in six minutes, through a gateway.

Keep left on reaching a gate at the end of a track coming from the right and make for the farm of Ruma Nou, which you will see ahead. Pass to the left of this pretty farm (**1h10min**) and, in two minutes, go through a gate. Continue with fine views over the valleys until, in six minutes, you go through two sets of gates and approach the farm of Sant Josep. Enter the farmyard via a gate, pass to the left of the house, and go through the gate on the right, adjacent to the house. Walk forward, with a wall to your left, on a fairly distinct path along the ridge. In five minutes go through a gap in a wall and cross the next field, with a wall now to your right. Make for a hill ahead, where you will see a white triangular marker. Go

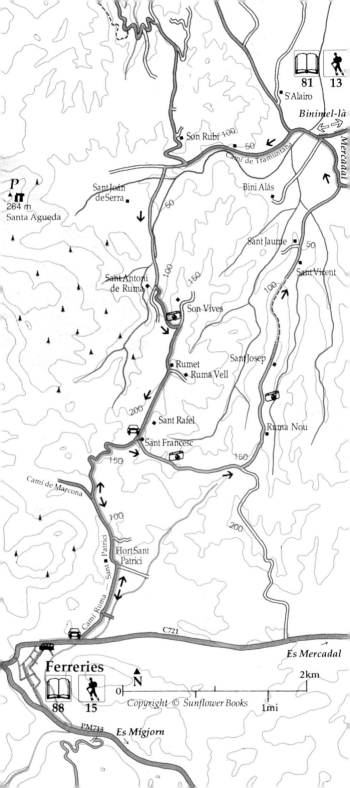

S'Alairo

Binimel-là

Mercadal

Son Rubí  100
50
Camí de Tramuntana

Bini Alás

P
264 m
Santa Agueda

Sant Joan
de Serra

50

Sant Jaume
50

Sant Vicent

Sant Antoni
de Ruma

100
150

Son Vives

100

Sant Josep

Rumet
Ruma Vell

Ruma Nou

200

Sant Rafel

Sant Francesc

150

150

Camí de Marcona

100

200

Sant Patrici

Hort Sant
Patrici

Camí Ruma

C721

Es Mercadal

Ferreries

N

2km

88  15

0

1mi

Copyright © Sunflower Books

PM713  Es Migjorn

through another gap and head towards a wall. The white marker is directly to your right now, beyond the bushes.

Turn left and walk beside the wall for 50m/yds, until you come to a small gate. Go through the gate and walk straight ahead, making your way round the hill until you can see two farms below you. Make your way downhill now, to the track leading to the nearer of them, Sant Vicent. Enter the yard by an iron gate and pass to the left of the farmhouse (**1h40min**). Continue your descent past the farm of Sant Jaume and, in ten minutes, having gone through three sets of iron gates, you will arrive at a junction with the metalled S'Alairo road from Es Mercadal (**1h55min**). Turn left.

In seven minutes (**2h02min**) ignore the sharp bend to the right, which leads to Binimel-là (*Longer walk and Picnic 12;* map page 81). Continue over a bridge (the Pont de S'Alairo). This surfaced road is signposted 'Camí de Tramuntana'. Follow it for 1.3km/0.8mi, in three minutes passing a stone track heading right between some cream-coloured pillars (**2h10min**) — the outgoing route of Walk 13. In 12 minutes you go by a deserted cottage and in 22 minutes you reach a track on the right, going up to Son Rubí (Walk 13 descends this track). The tarmac ends now. Keep to the left along the track and, in 250m/yds, turn left at the fork. In seven minutes, you pass the entrance to Sant Joan de Serra on the right. Keep straight on for Sant Antoni de Ruma, going through two sets of gates. Turn right and, having passed through another gateway, climb up towards the house, passing to the left of it.

Now (**2h55min**) turn left and follow an asphalted road quite steeply uphill, going through gates and continuing to climb for 11 minutes, until you reach the head of a valley. You could picnic here in the shade, enjoying the magnificent views. Shortly after this, pass through a gate and turn right. On your left is the entrance to Son Vives farm. The worst of the climbing is now behind you. In seven minutes pass the farms of Rumet and Ruma Vell on your left and, in another five minutes, Sant Rafel. Two minutes sees you back at Sant Francesc (**3h25min**), faced with a steep descent that some may find as uncomfortable as the climb. (*But the Shorter walk ends here.*) Bear left at the junction with the Camí de Marcona and follow the road between the allotments. Half an hour from Sant Francesc you will reach the main road. Turn right here and follow the main road back into Ferreries, where you will find your car or the bus stop, on your left (**4h05min**).

## 15 THE GORGES AND PREHISTORIC VILLAGE OF SON MERCER

**Distance:** 13.3km/8.3mi; 3h35min      **Grade:** strenuous

**Equipment:** walking boots or comfortable shoes or trainers, sunhat, raingear, suncream, picnic, plenty of water, long trousers

**How to get there and return:** 🚌 or 🚐 to/from Ferreries (park beside the main road or by the football ground in Carrer Formentera).

**Shorter walks** (grade, equipment, access as above)

1 Barranco de Sa Cova (10.5km/6.5mi; 2h57min). Follow the main walk as far as the 1h55min-point. Turn right here, and rejoin the main walk at the 2h33min-point.

2 Prehistoric village (11km/6.8mi; 2h41min; *note that boots and long trousers are not necessary*). Follow the main walk to the 41min-point but, instead of turning left, keep straight ahead in the direction of a farm building. Go through a gate and carry on until you reach Son Mercer de Baix farm. Cross the farmyard, and in three minutes, when you meet a track coming from the left, keep straight ahead and rejoin the main walk at the 1h55min-point.

T he farms of Son Mercer are situated on a small plateau entirely surrounded by precipitous cliffs and deep gorges, the *barrancos* of Trebalúger and Sa Cova, and the *torrente* of Son Gras. Such terrain is ideal for bird life. And also for defence. It was here, in one of the most unassailable positions on the island, that a group of talayotic people decided to build their village; the views they enjoyed are breathtaking, as you can see in the photograph opposite. Incidentally, the farms' name illustrates perfectly the multiplicity of Menorquín spellings. There are no less than four versions — Mercé, Marcé, Marcer, Mercer. I have chosen the last because it is on the farm gate.

**To begin the walk**, leave the bus stop and walk into Ferreries along Carrer Son Granot (the street on the left of the roundabout). Ahead you will see a hill with a small chapel on top.

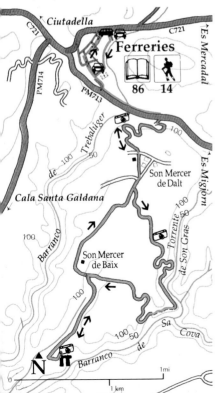

At the end of this short street turn right and walk round the edge of a concrete storm drain until you come to a school (on your left) and football ground (on your right). Turn right here, and walk beside the stadium along Carrer Formentera (where there are parking spaces). At the end turn left into Carrer Migjorn Gran, and on reaching a T-junction (PM713) turn left towards Es Migjorn (**11min**).

Six minutes after crossing the river bridge turn right up a sandy track signposted 'Poblat Son Marcé de Baix'. Go over a cattle grid and begin to climb the hill. In three minutes ignore a track on the left, and in a further 12 minutes, after passing some fine megaliths at the side of the road, you will arrive at the farm of Son Mercer de Dalt.

Turn right, and then keep straight ahead through a gateway, along a well-made but unsealed road, with farm buildings to your left and a lovely farmhouse on your right. In five minutes, having passed a slurry pit and gone through another gateway, ignore a track on the right. Some 100m/yds further on, turn left along a broad track (**41min**). *(But for Shorter walk 2, keep straight ahead.)* Eight minutes later the track turns right through a gateway and narrows. In four minutes go through another gateway: ahead is the valley of the Torrente de Son Gras.

*The Bronze Age settlement at Son Mercer de Baix is the best place on the island to view some of the deep valleys that gouge their way to the sea across southern Menorca. In this photograph the Barranco de Sa Cova leads the eye to Monte Toro in the distance.*

When the island was formed these valleys of southern Menorca did not exist. The land was level, but millions of years of rain storms have eroded them, and the process is still going on. A few years ago heavy storms washed away this track, hence the new track that you are now walking on (**1h**). After a while you will be back on the old track, and eight minutes' more walking will bring you to the valley floor.

Go through the gateway into a field. Early in the summer, if it is in crop, walk along the right-hand edge (but watch out for brambles). When the crop has been harvested it is easier. You pass into the second field via an overgrown gap in the wall. Keeping to the edge, cross the second field. The passage into field three is much easier, and at the end you exit through a gap into a short, walled-in track. Turn right, and in a few metres/ yards, turn left through a gate, cross the paved yard in front of the house, and leave through the gate opposite. Turn right, then left, and carry on along a good track above and to the right of a large orchard (**1h22min**).

You now climb back out of the valley. After some 20 minutes go through a gate (**1h44min**) and turn right through another one in 50m/yds, to cross a wide field. When, in three minutes, you pass through another gate, you will see the farm of Son Mercer de Baix ahead.

You pass through two more gates, in three and eight minutes, and come to the important junction shown opposite (**1h55min**), where the farm is to the right. Turn left. *(Shorter walk 1 turns right here; Shorter walk 2 comes in here and keeps straight ahead.)* Follow a wide walled-in

Besides telling of their skill with the sling, the writers of antiquity have left us other fascinating glimpses of the inhabitants of these prehistoric Menorcan towns. For example, one name for the islands was 'the Gymnesiae', given (according to one writer) 'because the inhabitants go about naked during the summer'. *Plus ça change ...* only perhaps we should change 'inhabitants' to 'visitors'. But if that is the case, we must hope that it does not apply equally to another of their customs: 'At the wedding the bride was first possessed by the friends and relations of the bridegroom in exchange for gifts'. One thing the writers all agree on — the warriors wore no armour in battle. In fact they had little time for metal. There was a ban on the import and use of gold and silver, of which none has been found by archaeologists, and the victorious warrior much preferred to take his spoil in women and wine. In fact they prized women highly, and if their women were carried off by enemies, they would make every effort to ransom them. Lacking gold, they would give three or four men of rank in exchange.

*This important junction is passed twice during the walk: at 1h55min and at 2h33min. The flat countryside beyond the typical Menorcan wooden gate is deceptive. Between the cowshed and the distant farms deep, steep-sided valleys cut through the landscape.*

track. After 20 minutes you arrive at the remains of a prehistoric village. Most of the buildings are little more than foundations, but there is one more intact with three pillars, typically wider at the top than the bottom, supporting the roof. For the best views walk up to the rear of the village and gaze eastwards over the Barranco de Sa Cova (**2h15min**; see photograph on page 89).

When you leave the village, retrace your steps past the track you climbed from the valley (**2h33min**), and cross the Son Mercer de Baix farmyard. In seven minutes go through a gate, and eight minutes later another. Pass some farm buildings on the left and then the track you took to descend into the valley (**2h53min**). Go by Son Mercer de Dalt and the megaliths, and descend the twisting track back to the main road (**3h10min**).

Turn left, then in ten minutes fork right into Ferreries. This time keep straight ahead when you come to the football ground, forking right to cross the little Plaça Menorca and going along Carrer Pau Pons. This brings you into the main square, the Plaça Espanya, where you turn right to follow the Avinguda Vergé del Toro back to the bus stop (**3h35min**).

See map pages 96-97; see also photographs pages 28-29

**Distance:** 8.5km/5.3mi; 2h46min

**Grade:** moderate; the section between Cala Mitjana and Trebalúger beach requires some agility and is *not recommended for small children*.

**Equipment:** walking boots or comfortable footwear, sunhat, raingear, suncream, picnic, plenty of water, swimwear, towel, binoculars

**How to get there and return:** 🚌 or 🚗 to/from Cala Santa Galdana. Travelling by bus, it may be necessary to go to Ferreries first. By car, at the roundabout at the entrance to the resort, take the middle road and turn right over the bridge. Park in the large car park on the right.

Perhaps because it is one of its loveliest bays, Cala Trebalúger is one of Menorca's most closely-guarded secrets. As beautiful as the beach is, where the valley behind it, where the gorges seen on Walk 15 finally meet the sea.

**Begin** by leaving the bus stop/car park in Cala Santa Galdana and making your way on to the beach. Facing the sea, turn left and cross to the far side where you will find a flight of steps. Climb to the top of the cliff, and in 20m/yds turn left along the road. In 100m/yds you will reach a car parking area. Turn right along a short street here, Camí d'es Cavalls (**20min**). Beyond the turning circle continue along a short track through a gate marked with a tiny red arrow. You will find these red waymarks most helpful. After 20m/yds the path divides. Fork left in the direction of houses and a stone wall. The path is waymarked at intervals. Within three minutes you pass the wreck of a red car, and not long afterwards go through a gap in the wall. Bear right now on a good track (heaps of stones deter cars). Two minutes later go over a crossing track, and after a similar interval walk diagonally to the right across an open space to join an even wider track. Bear right again and keep on this track, ignoring all minor paths and tracks to left and right, even when at one point the red dots appear to be trying to seduce you from it.

After twisting and turning for a couple of minutes the track passes a troglodytic dwelling on your right, and then continues downhill to the *calas*. There are two bays. The first, Cala Mitjaneta, shown opposite, is rocky. Keep on the track for 12 minutes more, to the rear of a large sandy beach, Cala Mitjana (**44min**; Picnic 10).

Walk diagonally left across the sand in the direction of the sea to a point about halfway along the far side of the beach. Where the rock of the cliff begins to slope up from the sand you will see a little red arrow. Leave the sand here, and walk along an upward sloping narrow rock ledge, parallel with the beach, in the direction of the sea, for about 40m/yds, passing a maritime zone marker similar to the one shown here.  Now the ledge broadens out, but you must veer left and start to climb upwards. At this point the path is fairly indistinct, but with luck you will see a red dot on your left after two or three paces. Keep climbing diagonally left, and after another two or three paces the narrow path becomes very distinct and well waymarked. Five minutes should see you at the top of the cliff, where a waymarked path leads you to a gap in a broken dry-stone wall. Ignore a track on your left, and follow the more worn track towards a pine tree bearing a red dot. In eight minutes ignore a track on the right, and turn left. Two minutes later fork left, pass a lime-kiln, and after 25m/yds turn right (**1h04min**).

The path cuts through two walls, and in four minutes emerges from the wood into a field. Walk beside the bushes on your right to the far side of the field and re-enter woodland. Climb over another, broken wall, and then, slowly at first, begin to descend. The last ten minutes of descent are quite steep, and the last few metres will have you scrambling. At high tide you will have to paddle across the end of the narrow river to reach the sand of a glorious bay, Cala Trebalúger (**1h25min**).

It is just possibly deserted. I say possibly, because it is visited by boats bringing holidaymakers for a barbecue lunch. You will also find plenty of open space shaded by pine trees, where you can picnic. Before leaving the beach, walk away from the sea and through the wood to look out over the river at the end of the valley. Not only is the view most attractive but, if you are lucky, you may

*Cala Mitjaneta*

also see one of Menorca's most attractive birds, the bee-eater, which nests here. If not you should at least see a heron as some kind of consolation.

You must now retrace your steps to return to Cala Santa Galdana. Near to the water's edge you will see, on the far side of the river, a large prehistoric cave. To the left of it you will also see a small stone pillar or stump, maybe a 2ft cube, marked with a red dot. That is where you must begin your ascent, climbing to the left. You have about 15m/yds to scramble before reaching the tree-line, from where the path is clear and the climb easy.

Ten minutes after leaving the beach you climb over a broken wall into a pine wood. You soon leave it again and enter a field. Walk across open ground to bushes ahead, and follow the track to the right of them until you are back in woodland. After about four minutes you come to a T-junction where you turn left, pass the lime-kiln, and turn right, ignoring a track to the left (**1h44min**). Two minutes later the track forks. Go right, and in eight minutes go through a broken wall and you will be at the top of the cliff and ready for a steep descent down the narrow waymarked path, back to Cala Mitjana (**2h**).

Walk diagonally to the back of the beach, pass some boulders and go along a track as it bends to the left and starts to climb. After 100m/yds, when it joins another track, turn sharp left. You climb now, heading towards the sea, and will pass the end of Cala Mitjaneta. Ignore a track going to the left along the side of this bay, and climb a waymarked track uphill. Where you bend right in front of the cave, ignore the track to the right. Indeed, ignore all turnings to left and right until, 15 minutes after leaving the beach, you arrive at an open space on your left with some building remains on the far side. Leave the track now, and walk diagonally across this space. Pass through a gap in a wall and shortly go over a crossing track. In two minutes, just beyond a heap of stones, turn left through a gap in the wall. After the red car you must concentrate: in about three minutes you must turn right along the short path leading to the metal gate (it is very easy to miss this path). Beyond the gate a short track brings you to a metalled road (**2h26min**) .

At the end of the road turn left, and after 100m/yds turn right. You arrive at the head of the flight of steps that take you back down to Cala Santa Galdana. Make your way towards the far side of the bay, cross the river bridge, and turn right, back to the bus stop/car park (**2h46min**).

## 17 CALA SANTA GALDANA • TORRE TRENCADA • CALA MACARELLA • CALA SANTA GALDANA

**See also photograph pages 28-29**

**Distance:** 20.2km/12.5mi; 5h20min  **Grade:** moderate

**Equipment:** comfortable footwear, sunhat, raingear, suncream, picnic, plenty of water, swimwear, towel

**How to get there and return:** 🚌 or 🚗 to/from Cala Santa Galdana. Travelling by bus, it may be necessary to go to Ferreries first. By car, at the roundabout at the entrance to the resort, take the middle road and turn right over the bridge. Park in the large car park on the right.

**Shorter walks** (grade, equipment, access as main walk)

1 Barranco de Cala Santa Galdana (6km/3.8mi; 1h30min). Follow the main walk to the 50min-point. Turn left here, and walk along a track away from Santa Galdana farmhouse — the track curls round the edge of the field you have just crossed. Continue on this track for 20min, walking more or less south, until it forks by a farm, the Estancia de Son Mestres. Go left now, and continue as before, but soon going downhill. In 10 minutes you will be back at the 13min-point in the main walk. Turn right and retrace your steps back to the car park and bus stop.

2 Barranco de Macarella (13km/8.1mi; 3h30min). See page 98.

---

Walk up the *barranco* of Cala Santa Galdana while the birds are singing, have lunch around a megalithic table in a Bronze Age village, enjoy the beauty of Macarella's valley, refresh yourselves on its beach, and finally walk beneath pines back to Cala Santa Galdana.

*In October the track from Cala Santa Galdana to Cala Macarella is garlanded with autumn crocuses, in spring with asphodel.*

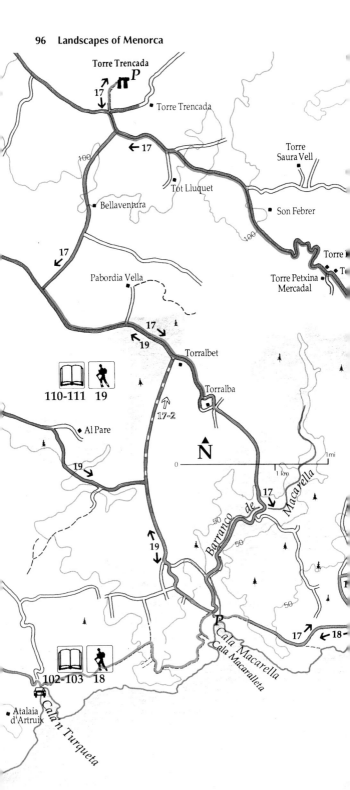

**Start the walk** at the bus stop/car park at Cala Santa Galdana: turn right and walk away from the sea. *(But Shorter walk 2 goes left here.)* Follow the road beside the car park. Ahead is a splendid palm tree, beyond which the metalled road gives way to gravel track. In 10 minutes you reach a padlocked gate; climb over the wall at the right. Three minutes later (**13min**) the track divides. *(Shorter walk 1 comes in from the left here.)* Take the lower track on the right and carry on along the valley floor. In seven minutes climbing, on coming to a second gate, climb over the wall at the side of it. Six minutes later the track forks round a large bush: the most-used track enters a field, but your way is the more overgrown track to the left, and you begin to climb out of the valley. Fourteen minutes beyond the fork, climb over a barrier made of wooden pallets (carefully, because you do not want the cows to get out) and turn right. The track swings round to the left beside a wall, and ahead you can see the farm of Santa Galdana. Follow the track across the field to the gate at the left of the farm buildings (**50min**). *(Shorter walk 1 goes left here.)*

Walk straight ahead now, with the farmhouse on your right, passing a cowshed on your left, and going beneath power lines. At the end of the farm drive

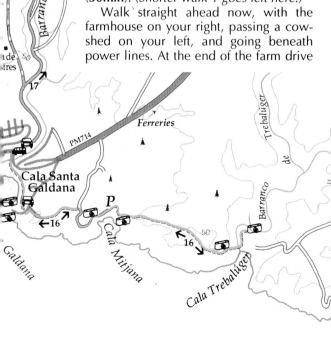

---

**Shorter walk 17-2: Barranco de Macarella**

On leaving the bus stop or car park in Cala Santa Galdana, turn left and walk along the road towards the sea, keeping to the right of the river. Ahead of you, beyond the Hotel Audax, climb steps to the foot of the cliff. From here follow a footpath past the end of a small bridge and up the side of the cliff between pine trees. In five minutes go through a gap in a wall, and very shortly turn left along a wide track. For the next 12 minutes you will have the dry-stone wall immediately to your right.

Five minutes after passing through the gap the track crosses the end of a little valley, forks left, and passes a fire risk warning sign. You will notice that there are yellow daubs on the trees which act as waymarks, and also small red dots. Immediately after the fire risk notice, climb over some rocks and turn right along a wide track, still beside the wall. In a couple of minutes do something similar, and two minutes after that begin to walk away from the wall. Some 33 minutes into the walk the track turns right, shrinks to a path, and descends steeply to Cala Macarella, often on steps cut from the rock. The way is shown by yellow paint daubs. Finally the path levels out and takes you past the end of the garden of the Cafeteria Susy.

Cross to the far side of the beach and turn right at the foot of the cliff. You will come to an iron gate. Ignore the green arrow and track to the left, and go past the gate. Follow the track beyond the gate uphill. In 15 minutes turn right, away from a large house. Ignore a track on the right and go through a gate. There are red dot waymarks. When you come to a T-junction, turn right and head north for 10 minutes. You now have to climb over a fairly high wall to avoid a padlocked gate (the 1h23min-point in Walk 19). Keep straight ahead for 22 minutes, pass the farm of Torralbet, and emerge on a tarmac road. Turn right and pick up the notes opposite, at the 3h28min-point.

---

climb over another gate and turn right on a metalled country lane. There will be little traffic because it leads nowhere. (Any cars you meet will probably be driven by tourists unaware of this!) In eight minutes, when the lane turns left, you will see on the hill in front the three farms of Torre Petxina: Nova, Vella, and Mercadal. As you walk up to the farms, the hill to your right is Puig de Santa Magdalena (137m/450ft).

Beyond the farms you cross a valley, and climb to pass Torre Petxina school and the entrance to Son Febrer farm (**1h48min**). In four minutes, as you pass under power lines, ignore a road on the right. You will pass the entrance to Tot Lluquet farm in 13 minutes, and nine minutes later a gated track on the left with a notice saying 'Camino Particular' (private road; **2h14min**). You will be returning along this track after visiting the prehistoric settlement ahead. Two minutes later you will be in the little parking area provided for visitors to the site, from where a signposted path leads across the fields to the settlement of Torre Trencada (**2h24min**; Picnic 13).

To continue the walk, return to the car park and turn left. Ignore the road on the left to Torre Trencada farm, and walk straight ahead until you come to the track labelled 'Camino Particular'. Turn right along this track. It is barred to traffic for otherwise it would provide a short-cut for cars from the Ferreries/Ciutadella highway to the southern beaches, enabling them to avoid Ciutadella.

In nine minutes pass farm buildings, and four minutes come to a gateway blocked off by a loosely-built dry-stone wall. Do not try to climb over the loose stones which will probably collapse beneath you. Climb over the solidly-built wall at the side. Cross the narrow field at the side of Bellaventura farm and turn right (**2h50min**). Six minutes later ignore a track on the left. In a further nine minutes turn left when you reach the road. (Walk 19 follows this road west to Sant Joan de Missa.) Having passed the track to Pabordia Vella, you will come to the farm of Torralbet in **3h28min**.

Continue to follow the road for for seven minutes, when the asphalt stops, and the track forks. Take the track to the left signposted 'Macarella', which bypasses the farm of Torralba. Go through a gate, over a cattle grid, and keep straight ahead. In 10 minutes the track starts to descend quite steeply into the valley. It is wooded and shaded now, spoiled only by the dust thrown up by the far too many cars making for Cala Macarella, which you will reach in rather more than half an hour after leaving Torralba farm (**4h14min**; Picnic 11). Walks 18 and 19 also visit this beach.

You will be grateful now for the Cafeteria Susy beside the beach, where you can rest and refresh yourselves. To continue your walk, go through a metal gate next to the seaward end of the cafeteria's garden. Begin a steep, but fairly easy, ascent of the cliff, at times using steps cut from the rock. The route to Cala Santa Galdana is clearly waymarked with yellow daubs on trees and rocks. After six minutes the path reaches the cliff top and veers left, broadening into a wide track.

Nothing much happens for the next quarter of an hour, but then the track forks. You must turn left, clambering down over rocks, keeping beside a wall on your left as you have done since the path reached the top of the cliff. Two minutes later do something similar. There is a red dot on a tree as well as the yellow waymarks, and you will also pass a notice warning you not to light fires. During the next eight minutes ignore occasional paths to the right, and continue to follow the wide track beside the wall.

When you come to a gap in the wall turn left along a narrow path (**4h44min**). In 20m/yds turn right along a good track. Walk through a pine wood for seven minutes until you come to a T-junction when you turn right. In six minutes turn right when the track forks, and six minutes later you will pass through a gate and there is Cala Santa Galdana before you (**5h03min**). Turn left and follow the road round to the right. Almost at once go down steps on your right, and go down to the bay past the Hotel Audax. Turn left once more, and walk round the bay to the car park and bus stop (**5h20min**).

*You could picnic here under the pines, overlooking Cala Santa Galdana (Shorter walk 17-2, Walk 18).*

# 18  A COASTAL WALK BETWEEN CALA'N BOSCH AND CALA SANTA GALDANA

See also photographs opposite and pages 15, 28-29, 95

Maps on pages 96-97, 102-103                    **Grade:** moderate

**Equipment:** comfortable footwear, sunhat, raingear, suncream, picnic, plenty of water, swimwear, towel

**Distance, How to get there and return:** See below and page 105

Sometimes winding through beautiful countryside, sometimes beside the sea, continually descending to breath-taking beaches, often following ancient tracks and passing ancient buildings, this walk may well prove to be many people's favourite. It is described fully in both directions. Since it is a long walk, you may wish to follow only part of it and then retrace your steps. (To make this easier, at each time check I have inserted, *in italics,* the time check if walking in the reverse direction.)

## From Cala'n Bosch to Cala Santa Galdana

**Distance:** 16km/10mi; 4h15min

**How to get there:** 🚌 to Cala'n Bosch (alight at the Cala'n Bosch Hotel). Or 🚗 (only possible if you intend to walk part way, and then to retrace your steps to Cala'n Bosch). Drive to Cala'n Bosch. Follow the PM721 nearly to the lighthouse at Cap d'Artruix and turn left. Drive by the sea and follow the road round to the left, where you will see a footbridge over the entrance to the marina. Park near the bridge, and walk over it to the Cala'n Bosch Hotel, to begin the walk.

*To return:* 🚌 from Cala Santa Galdana or 🚗 from Cala'n Bosch

**Begin the walk** by heading across Cala'n Bosch beach and climbing up to the headland on the far side. Walk round the headland (there are paths to follow) and you will arrive at a car park. Walk across to the adjacent bay, Son Xoriguer, and make your way round that as well. Pass a fork off to the left and carry on until you are nearly at the end of the far arm (**20min**) *(4h).* Look now for a sandy track also going away to the left. Turn along that track, soon skirting a dry-stone wall. The sea is never far away to your right, as the way takes you between bushes. After 0.5km/0.3mi a similar track goes off left, but ignore that, and continue to walk parallel with the sea. In 100m/yds you will come to a wall that goes down to the sea. Go through a gateway and shortly you will reach Cala Parejals. This is a forbidding place, much eroded by the sea and giving the impression that the whole cliff is about to collapse. It is watched over by a machine-gun post, the first of many military buildings and blockhouses along this coast. Pass a little white building, and soon afterwards go through a wooden gate (**45min**) *(3h35min).*

Continue with a wall to your left and Punta Prima to

your right. In six minutes go through a gap in a wall, ignore a path to the left, and walk across rocky ground towards bushes opposite. The path is barely discernible as it winds round the next seaweedy bay, Cala de Son Vell. Follow it round the back of bushes and start to go down to the little bay. Before you get there, turn left round a squatters' camp and go up an ancient track. The bedrock surface of this cart-track is deeply worn and rutted in places, testifying both to its antiquity and the volume of traffic which once made its way to this isolated bay in an age when the sea offered the easiest way of moving about the island. You pass a curious megalithic enclosure on the left and, in 100m/yds, arrive at a T-junction. Turn right here and follow the track for another 350m/yds until, 50m/yds before it reaches a wall, you turn right along a path which brings you to a gate lower down in the wall (**1h01min**) *(3h15min)*.

Beyond the gate, follow the path ahead, veering towards the sea. In a couple of minutes you pass between a pair of caves. The one on the right is worth exploring, since it is a good example of a Menorcan troglodyte home. The central pillar giving support to the roof, and the pilaster on the right, are common features.

The path continues eastwards until reaching wooded terrain. Pass between bushes on the left and the Pesquera d'es Conde on the seaward side. Where there is neither track nor footpath, Spanish law still gives you a right of way along the seashore. From the high water mark for six metres inland, all the coastline of Spain belongs to the state, and along this strip the walker has right of access (unless it has been appropriated by the military). The boundary of this maritime zone is indicated by small concrete markers inscribed 'TMZ' (see drawing on page 93).

Cross the end of a headland, beyond which is a little *cala*. Here your path joins a track which has come from the left (from Torre Saura Vell). Continue round the beach, past two blockhouses. In 200m/yds you will arrive at the Racó d'es Pi, with the beach of Son Saura in view. If you

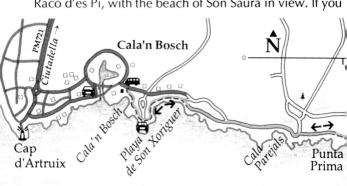

look straight across the bay, you will see another military post on a hilltop — the medieval watchtower of Artruix, shown on page 107. The path descends to sea level, crossing a slipway and passing another gun-post. Here you join another ancient cart-track. Ignore a path on the right and, when you come to a T-junction, turn right. Shortly, turn right again, to skirt to the right of a wall. Cross a small footbridge to reach the seaweedy Platja de Son Saura shown on page 15 (**1h40min**) *(2h30min)*.

Walk across the bay, but about 100m/yds before you reach the far side, watch for a path on your left and turn along it. After about 25m/yds it goes through a gap in a wall (the remains of a blockhouse; waymarked with a red dot). Beyond the gap, turn left and follow the path in a semicircle through woodland (where a terrible storm caused the havoc you see about you). The path takes you past yet another blockhouse and through a gateway. In nine minutes you arrive at a car park. Turn right and you come to a beautiful little beach, currently free of sea-weed, Cala d'es Talaier (**1h53min**) *(2h21min)*.

Return to the car park and turn right to continue along an unmetalled road, ignoring the chained-off track to the left. In eight minutes you will see a red iron gate ahead. The road bends left some 20m/yds short of it, but leave the road here and walk to the gate. Use the *botador* (stone steps) to climb over the wall, and at once fork right. In three minutes you will pass through a gap in a wall and the track will narrow to a footpath as it climbs up to the watchtower you saw earlier. At **2h11min** *(2h02min)* you stand at the foot of the Atalaia d'Artruix. With care you can climb to the top and enjoy wide-ranging views over the flattish countryside on this part of the island.

Retrace your steps but, when the track forks, do not go back to the iron gate; instead keep straight ahead in the direction of the lovely cream-coloured Mallauí farm-house that you saw from the top of the tower. Four minutes after passing by the iron gate you come to a junction. Turn

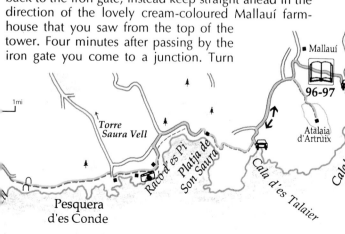

right, and follow the ancient track from the farm down to Turqueta beach. In seven minutes pass through a gap in a wall into an open area, from which several paths radiate. Turn left and walk along the edge of this space with bushes immediately to your left for 20m/yds, then go through another gap on to a crossing track. Turn left and carry on through the pine wood. Very soon you will begin to descend to the beach. On reaching the car park, turn right and walk beneath the shade of pines to the beach of Cala'n Turqueta (**2h37min**) *(1h36min)*.

You will have no difficulty in finding the path you leave by on the opposite side of the beach, towards the rear. But it is not the track you came on, and you do not have to go through the car park to get to it. For a few minutes you climb through a pine wood, before emerging into more open country. Now the path bends left; here ignore a path on the right. For five minutes the path winds through low bushes before coming to a wall, where you pass through a gateway. Keep straight ahead now, with a wall on your left. After another seven minutes the path has widened and brought you to a T-junction, where you turn right (**2h59min**) *(1h13min)*. Shortly, ignore two paths on the right, and start to go downhill through the small valley that brings you to another superb little beach and *cala*, Macarelleta (**3h09min**) *(56min)*.

You have in the course of this walk travelled along several ancient tracks and paths, but none more ancient than the one by which you will leave this bay. If you cross to the left hand side (as you face the sea) of the beach, you will see steps cut into the rock, which turn left and wind their way up to the top of the cliff. Ascend by these steps which were cut out in prehistoric times, and which in the Middle Ages were mostly used by pirates. From the top of the steps a short path leads to a T-junction with a good track. Your way is left, but before leaving, walk in the opposite direction to the end of the headland where you have splendid views over both Macarelleta beach and its larger neighbour, Macarella.

Retrace your steps and pass the little path. Two minutes later, when the track turns right, ignore a track on the left, and in 50m/yds turn right down a rocky path. Go through a gap in a wall, and keep descending until you emerge at the rear of Macarella beach (**3h27min**) *(40min)*. Walk across the beach, setting for Picnic 11 (and also visited in Walks 17 and 19). On the opposite side is a fine beach bar and restaurant, the Cafeteria Susy (open from late April to October). Its garden stretches towards the sea, and where it ends there is a metal gate. To continue the walk, go through that gate and begin a steep, but fairly easy, ascent of the cliff, at times using steps not unlike the ones you met at Macarelleta beach. The route to Cala Santa Galdana is clearly waymarked with yellow daubs on trees and rocks. In six minutes the path reaches the cliff top and veers left, broadening into a wide track.

Some 13 minutes along the track forks. Turn left, clambering down over rocks, skirting a wall on your left (as you have done since the path reached the top of the cliff). Two minutes later do something similar. There is a red dot on a tree as well as the yellow waymarks, and you will also pass a fire warning. During the next eight minutes ignore occasional paths to the right, and continue to follow the wide track beside the wall. When you come to a gap in the wall (**4h**) *(15min)* ignore the track to the left, and follow the stony path down the side of the cliff towards Cala Santa Galdana (photographs pages 28-29, 100). Soon you will pass the end of a bridge and go down steps to the road beside the Hotel Audax. Follow the road beside the river towards a large car park just beyond the main road bridge over the river. The bus stop is next to the car park (**4h15min**).

## Cala Santa Galdana to Cala'n Bosch

**Distance:** 16km/10mi; 4h25min
**How to get there:** 🚌 to Cala Santa Galdana. It may be necessary to go to Ferreries first. Or 🚗 (only possible if you intend to walk part way and then re-trace your steps to Cala Santa Galdana). Drive to Cala Santa Galdana. At the roundabout as you enter the resort, take the middle road down into the town and turn right over the bridge. Park in the large car park on the right.
*To return:* 🚌 from Cala'n Bosch or 🚗 from Cala Santa Galdana

Leaving the bus stop or car park in Cala Santa Galdana, turn left, and **begin** by walking along the road towards the sea, keeping to the right of the river. Ahead of you, beyond the Hotel Audax, steps take you to the foot of the cliff and to a footpath which climbs past the end of a small bridge and up the side of the cliff in the setting shown on pages 28-29 and 100. In five minutes go through a gap in a wall (**15min**) *(4h),* and very shortly turn left along a wide track. For the next 12 minutes you will skirt to the left of the dry-stone wall.

Five minutes after passing through the gap the track (photograph page 95) crosses the end of a little valley, forks left, and passes a fire risk warning sign. Yellow daubs on the trees act as waymarks, together with small red dots. The dots will prove helpful to you at critical moments for the whole of this walk. Immediately after the fire risk notice, climb over some rocks and turn right along a wide crossing track, still beside the wall. In a couple of minutes do something similar, and two minutes after that begin to walk away from the wall. After 10 minutes the track turns right, shrinks to a path, and descends steeply, often on steps cut from the rock. The path levels out at Cala Macarella, setting for Picnic 11 and also visited on Walks 17 and 19. You pass the end of the garden of a fine beach bar and restaurant, Cafeteria Susy, open from late April to October (**40min**) *(3h27min)*.

Cross the beach and go over the water drain. You will meet a number of similar water courses, which prevent the ends of the *barrancos* being marshes. To your left you will notice, halfway up the cliff face and overlooking the sea, a couple of caves and the wide ledge that leads to them — doubtless highly desirable residences in Menorca's troglodytic period. You will very soon meet more of their occupants' work. To your right, at the foot of the cliff, is an iron gate barring access to a track and bearing a green arrow. This points to a second track, immediately to the left of the gate, which otherwise would be hidden. Its great age is evident by the depth to which it is eroded. Walk up this track away from Macarella beach, and in two minutes pass through a gap in a wall.

Carry on ahead, ignoring a path on the left in two minutes. In another two minutes you will reach a T-junction. Here turn left and, 50m/yds further on, fork left. Follow this track to the end of the headland (about 200m/yds), for the views you get over two *calas.* Then retrace your steps for 50m/yds and turn left along a narrow path (red waymarks). The path goes straight to the edge of the cliff, where a stone staircase has been cut from the rock by which you descend to Cala Macarelleta's little gem of a beach. These steps were cut by the denizens of those caves you saw earlier. Or if not by them, then by their prehistoric neighbours (**56min**) *(3h09min)*.

If you can bear to leave Cala Macarelleta, walk to the left of the back of the beach, and up a gravel track along the side of a small valley. Ignore a sandy track on the right. After ten minutes further walking there is a section of eroded track that has been repaired with concrete, and just beyond it two paths go off to your left. Ignore those, but, a minute later, turn left along a well-trodden path.

*Atalaia d'Artruix*

When last I saw it, there was no red dot waymark, but an arrow of stones indicated the way (**1h13min**) *(2h59min)*. Two buildings can be seen ahead, and you will have an opportunity to examine them more closely: the medieval watchtower of Artruix, and the cream-coloured Mallauí farmhouse. Nine minutes later the path goes through a gap in a wall, and in five minutes forks. Turn right along the wider path, descend through woodland, and finally emerge on the beach of Cala'n Turqueta (**1h36min**) *(2h37min)*.

To continue the walk, make your way to the track running along the left-hand side of the car park at the rear of the beach. Halfway along, turn left on a track which climbs into the pine wood. *Concentrate now!* In about three minutes you must leave this track and turn right on a path which goes through a gap in a dry-stone wall (easily missed). Beyond the gap is a largish open space. Walk round the right-hand edge at the side of the bushes and in 20m/yds turn right through another gap in the wall. *Ignore* all paths which leave this space to the left.

You are again on a good track, and in three minutes will pass through another gap in a wall. Five minutes after that you come to a junction. The track you are on swings right to the farm of Mallauí which you saw earlier, but you now turn left, in the direction of the watchtower. Soon you will see the track on the right leading to a red iron gate along which you will proceed after visiting the tower, but for now your way is forward for 10 minutes, until you come to the tower shown above — the Atalaia d'Artruix (**2h02min**) *(2h11min)*. At the moment it is still possible to climb it, but take care. The views from it are quite extensive over the flat countryside.

Return to the junction, turn left and climb the wall by the iron gate using the protruding stone steps. In 20m/yds you join a gravel road used by cars that has bypassed Mallauí. Keep straight ahead here. In nine minutes you will come to a car park. Walk between the car park and the sea, then turn left and go down to another lovely little beach, that of Cala d'es Talaier (**2h21min**) *(1h53min)*.

Retrace your steps to the car park, turn left and shortly go through a gate. Follow a sandy path for six minutes, then fork left and proceed in a semicircle past storm-felled trees. A minute later turn right through a gap in a wall (the remains of a blockhouse), to reach the Platja de Son Saura (**2h30min**) *(1h40min)*. This large beach, shown on page 15, was once the most beautiful on the coast, but in recent years it has been badly affected by seaweed.

When you are ready to leave Son Saura beach, walk round the edge towards the rock outcrop on the far side, and cross another marsh-draining water course. Follow the track beside a wall, turn left, and very shortly turn left again. Ignore a path on the left, and continue along an ancient cart track which runs to an old slipway. Cross the slipway, and follow a path for 200m/yds to the next bay. Walk round this bay, which is guarded at both ends by blockhouses, then make your way across the rocky headland and on between a wooded area on your right and the sea on your left. As you continue westwards across this rocky terrain you will pass between a pair of caves. The one on the left is rather nice, with a pilaster and central pillar. Two minutes beyond the caves, go through a gateway (**3h15min**) *(1h01min)*.

Veer right now, walking obliquely away from the wall for a minute, then turn left on a good track. Follow it inland for six minutes, then turn left down another ancient track leading to the sea. In 100m/yds look out for a small megalithic enclosure on your right, and follow the track round past a squatters' summer camp. Do not go all the way down to the sea, but turn right and follow the path round the back of bushes and across more rocky ground towards a wall. Ignore the path on the right, and go through a gap in the wall, to continue with a wall to your right and Punta Prima to your left. In six minutes go through a wooden gate (**3h35min**) *(45min)*.

Pass a small white building, then Cala Parejals, where the cliffs are steadily crumbling into the sea. Pass through a gateway and walk parallel with the sea for 100m/yds. Ignore a track to the right, and for another 0.5km/0.3mi walk between bushes with the sea on your left, to arrive at the beach of Son Xoriguer (**4h**) *(20min)*. Round the beach and leave the car park at the far end by a path in the right-hand corner (by the wall of a house). This will bring you to the final beach, at Cala'n Bosch. On the far side stands the Cala'n Bosch Hotel. Walk past it to the bus stop in front of the hotel entrance (**4h25min**).

# 19 ES PUJOL DE SON TICA AND CALA MACARELLA

**Distance:** 16km/10mi; 4h          **Grade:** moderate

**Equipment:** comfortable footwear, sunhat, raingear, suncream, picnic, plenty of water, swimwear, towel

**How to get there and return:** 🚗 The walk is only accessible by car. Drive to Ciutadella, turn left at the roundabout as you reach the town, following signs for the beaches of Macarella and Turqueta. After 5km you will see to your left the Ermita de Sant Joan de Missa shown on page 111. Park at the rear of the church.

**Shorter walks**

1  Es Pujol de Son Tica (12km/7.4mi; 3h; grade, access/return as main walk; equipment as main walk, less swimwear and towel). This version omits Cala Macarella. Follow the main walk to the 1h23min-point, then turn left and pick up the notes again at the 2h23min-point.

2  Sant Joan de Missa — Cala Macarella — Cala Santa Galdana (10km/6.3mi; 2h45min). Grade, equipment as main walk. Access: 🚗 taxi from Ciutadella to the Ermita de Sant Joan de Missa. Follow the main walk to the 1h53min-point. Then turn to page 104 and follow Walk 18 from the 3h27min-point to the end (map pages 96-97). Return by 🚌 from Cala Santa Galdana to Ciutadella (via Ferreries).

This walk, partly through agricultural country and partly through woodland, starts at the picturesque country church (*ermita*) of Sant Joan de Missa (St John the Baptist). It circles a region known as Es Pujol de Son Tica and visits a very beautiful beach.

**To begin**, leave the church and turn right, walking back briefly in the direction of Ciutadella. At the junction, turn left along the Camí de Son Camaro. In **10min** you pass the entrance to the farm of Son Focu on the left, and the tarmac road bends to the right. Leave the road here and follow the track to the left. At this point, the walk is interesting, but hardly exciting, as you make your way through flat pastures, passing the farm entrances of Son Tica and Lloc Nou. There now follows a gentle climb up to another farm, Son Piris (**35min**), beyond which the track descends into increasingly wooded and pretty countryside. Lovely bird-song accompanies you here.

Some **50min** after leaving the *ermita* you pass the gate to Marjaleta farm and climb slowly, to go through the gate of Al Pare. Now you only have a wall on your right. Soon you will see in the field to your right one of the island's characteristic cattle sheds, looking like the miniature Babylonian ziggurat with its stepped sides shown here. Since Menorca totally lacks building timber, all roofing until recent times was done with stones, hence the need to narrow the span to be covered in this imaginative and un- usual way.

Some eight minutes beyond the gate, go through another gateway to see the farm of Al Pare ahead through the trees. In three minutes turn right through a gate (red arrow) and follow the track across a field. (The track you have left leads to the farmhouse.) Go through another gate similarly waymarked, round the edge of a field and down beside a wall. On a distant hill ahead you can see the watchtower of Artruix visited on Walk 18.

Go through another gate and downhill, with a wall on your right, for 100m/yds, whereupon the track bends left. A quarter of an hour after turning away from Al Pare, you come to a wall (**1h12min**). Climb over *with care*, and follow the track across a field to the left, to a junction of tracks. Turn left here and go through another gate marked with a red arrow. Follow the track across four fields. Nine minutes later (**1h23min**), you will come to a T-junction. *(Shorter walk 1 turns left here.)* Turn right here, and climb over a fairly high wall beside a padlocked gate. *Referring now to the map on pages 96-97,* follow the track south for ten minutes, then turn left. Shortly, go through a gate and ignore a track on the left. At the next junction, do not approach the entrance to a large house, but turn left to continue south. The track, a very ancient one now, descends for 15 minutes. Walk past the gate at the bottom of the track, to emerge at Cala Macarella (**1h53min**; Picnic 11), also visited on Walks 17 and 18. *(Shorter walk 17-2 joins here.)* From late April to October you will find sustenance at Cafeteria Susy.

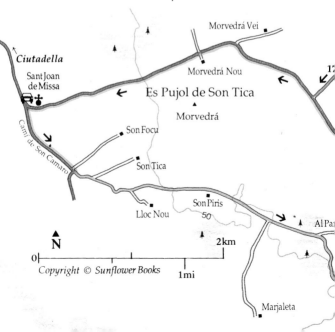

*The Ermita de Sant Joan de Missa seems to have been built shortly after the Reconquest of Menorca from the Moors by Alfonso III in 1287. It occupies an important place in local folklore. Every year the people of Ciutadella celebrate the birthday of St John the Baptist on 24th June with splendid displays of horsemanship in which more than 100 riders take part. The ceremonies begin on the eve of the festival, with all the horsemen riding out to this church to sing the evening service.*

From here retrace your steps to the high wall first encountered at 1h23min: turn right at the foot of the cliff, pass the iron gate and follow the track uphill. In 15 minutes turn right, away from the house. Ignore a track on the right and go through a gate. When you come to a T-junction, turn right and head north for 10 minutes. Climb back over the high wall (**2h23min**) and go forward, with a wall on your right. *(Shorter walk 1 rejoins here.)*

*Again referring to the map below,* at the top of the field you cross a cattle grid into the woodland. On a hot day the pines provide welcome shade. After seven minutes go through a gate and leave the wood. A good track takes you to the farm of Torralbet. Pass through two gates and

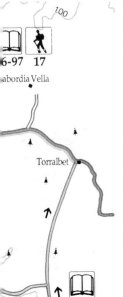

walk to the left of the farm, to a green iron gate (the 3h28min-point in Walk 17). Then turn left along the tarmac road (**2h45min**). In 10 minutes you pass the gate to Pabordia Vella on the right. Beyond here the pine woods on your left decline, and the road swings down and right to cross a low valley. After climbing out, the road bends left and eventually you pass the entrance to Morvedrá Vei (**3h25min**). Again the road turns left, in five minutes passing Morvedrá Nou. From the top of the hill Sant Joan de Missa can be seen. It is all downhill now and in 25 minutes you arrive back at the *ermita* (**4h**).

# 20 A WALKABOUT TOUR OF CIUTADELLA

**See town plan on pages 114-115 and photograph on page 122**

**Distance:** 3.3km/2mi; 2h                                    **Grade:** easy

**Equipment:** comfortable shoes of any sort, sunhat, raingear, suncream

**How to get there and return:** 🚌 or 🚗 to/from Ciutadella. Visitors arriving on the TMSA 🚌 from the Mahón direction or the mini-bus service from Cala Morell, should begin the tour at [1]. Those coming in from the beaches on the Torres 🚌 may find it more convenient to start at [2], page 116. By car, park in the Born Square, and start at [2].

The dismantling of the city walls was begun in 1868, so that 'the Citadel' could expand. Their line is marked by a series of wide tree-bedecked avenues which divide the old city from the modern part. Our walk lies entirely within the confines of the old city, which is where the most impressive and important buildings are to be found. Care must be taken to follow the route exactly as described, for it meanders through the maze of narrow streets which give Ciutadella its very special character, wherein aristocrat and artisan live side by side.

**The walk begins** in the Plaça d'Alfons III. Those of you coming from the Mahón bus depot should follow Carrer Barcelona to the main road (the Camí de Maó, along which the bus has just come) and turn left. The square will then be facing you beyond the traffic lights, looking quite French with its cafés. If you have come on the Cala Morell mini-bus, turn left as you get off the bus, pass Carrer Dormidor Monges on the right, and walk along the Avinguda de la Constitució for 100m/yds.

[1] The square is named after King Alfonso III of Aragon, nicknamed 'the Liberal', the hero of the Reconquest. Before 1868 the gate to the Old City stood on this spot. To left and right, where there are wide avenues today, the massive city walls rose up. Here Alfonso entered Ciutadella in triumph, and every 22nd January that event is celebrated. A statue of St Anthony Abad (on whose feast five days earlier the Moors had been vanquished) is carried in a cortège led by three horsemen. One of them bangs on the ground three times with his staff at the entrance to the city, to announce the King's arrival.

On the opposite side of the square from the Camí de Maó is the Carrer de Maó. This is the beginning of the main street through the town. Before starting along it, turn round and look back at the corner of the Camí de Maó, where a windmill has been turned into a popular bar. One of the chief attractions of Ciutadella is apparent as you walk between the houses which frame the entrance to Carrer de Maó — its many elegant buildings.

## About the city

As far as the British were concerned, Menorca was an appendage to Port Mahón. Most other rulers of the island preferred the harbour of Ciutadella. Although by no means so deep nor so long as that of Mahón, the port of Ciutadella was adequate for the shallow draught shipping of former times, and it had the advantage of being nearer both to Mallorca and mainland Spain. So it was here that the largest fortified city of the island grew up, hence its name 'Citadel'.

The history of the city begins in the time of the Carthaginians, who knew it as Iamno. In 123BC, Quintus Caecilius Metellus was sent by the Senate of Rome to suppress the Balearic pirates, which was sufficient excuse for him to add the islands to the Roman Empire (and reward himself by taking the title 'Balearicus'). Ciutadella changed its name slightly to Iamona, and 140km (85mi) of roads were built across Menorca to link it with other Roman forts at Santa Agueda and Mahón. The first Islamic raid occurred as early as 707, when Moorish pirates came in search of slaves, but the conquest of Menorca was delayed for two more centuries, until it was added to the Emirate of Cordova in 902. The Kaid, as the Muslim governor was called, chose Ciutadella to be his capital. He built his palace, the Alcazar, overlooking the harbour. For nearly four centuries the Moors knew the city by the Arabic name of Medina Minurka — 'The City of Menorca', and here they built their chief mosque. At the Reconquest in 1287 Alfonso III of Aragon entered Ciutadella on 22nd January and declared it the island's capital. Throughout the remainder of the Middle Ages there was continual rivalry between Ciutadella and Mahón, as the latter grew steadily in importance.

The most momentous event in Ciutadella's history took place in the year 1558, when 150 Turkish ships under the command of Barbarossa's successor Piali, carrying 15,000 troops, sailed into the port. After nine days' siege the city fell. Its 3495 inhabitants, including the governor Don Bartolome Arguimbau, were taken as slaves to Constantinople, and the city was sacked so completely that when a new governor came out, he was compelled to spend his first night in a cave — there were no houses left standing in Ciutadella.

But the city was rebuilt, and many of the captives were ransomed and returned home. However, even before the coming of the British in 1708, the governor moved his residence to Mahón, which served to intensify the rivalry between the two cities.

Some pleasant shops are to be found in Carrer de Maó, before it opens out into the delightful Plaça Nova. Walk along the left-hand side of the square, and continue into the narrow Ses Voltes (also called J M Quadrado; illustration at right), bordered on each side with arcades. These arches *(voltes)* are a feature of Ciutadella. At the end of Ses Voltes you come to Plaça de Pio XII (Plaça de la Catedral on most plans).

Carry on in the same direction, passing St Mary's

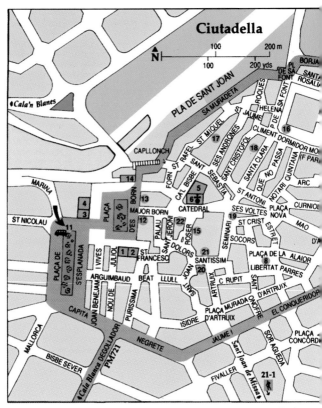

Cathedral on your right. This was where the Moors built their principal mosque. As soon as Alfonso expelled them, the mosque was consecrated as a Christian church, as were all other mosques on the island. Gradually a new Christian church was built to replace it, being completed in 1362. All that remains today of the Moorish building is part of the minaret, which was incorporated into the tower on the north side. The church is enclosed within a windowless curtain wall, which may be part of the original building or may have been added after the Turkish destruction to provide extra defence. So damaged was the building at that time that restoration took 150 years. The contrasting west entrance is a neo-classical addition dating from 1813. The interior suffered badly from vandalism at the hands of the Republicans during the Civil War. The tourist information office is on your left.

From the square keep going in the same westerly direction along Carrer Major del Born, which leads into

one of the finest city squares in the whole of Spain: the Plaça d'es Born (see illustration page 122). Dominating the square, a great obelisk commemorates the brave resistance put up by the townspeople to the Turkish attack. The Latin inscription (by Josep María Quadrado) translates 'Here we fought until death for our religion and our country in the year 1558'.

Turn left on leaving Major del Born and pass on the corner one of the most impressive mansions in Ciutadella, the Salort Palace. In summer, it is often open to visitors between 10am and 2pm. Remember to look upwards: here in Menorca the principal reception rooms are always on the first floor. The great wooden doors at ground level usually open on to spacious courtyards.

Continue your walk round the square until you reach the building opposite. To the left of it a passage leads to steps up to a *mirador* or viewpoint over the harbour. Today the building houses the police station and town

hall *(ajuntament)*. Once it was the governor's palace. The present building (see left) is the result of a 19th-century restoration. Its crenellation and round arches, and the palm trees in front, give this corner of Ciutadella a deliberately Moorish appearance: it was here that the Alcazar, the palace of the Kaid, stood for 385 years. Do go inside. Much can be seen, even during working hours. There is a Gothic reception hall with panelled ceiling and wrought iron lamps, a small museum which contains the battle banner of King Alfonso, and portraits of the city's notable citizens of yester-year (as well as one of King George III, which the British left behind, and another of the American admiral, David Farragut). After working hours, from 6-8pm (12-1pm on Saturdays) more of the rooms can be viewed. In the mayor's office is the 'Llibre Vermell', the medieval 'Red Book', recording the privileges King Alfonso gave to the island.

Facing you across the Born now, to the left of Carrer Major del Born, is the most splendid of all the houses in Ciutadella — the palace of the Count of Torre-Saura. The family coat-of-arms is emblazoned above the doorway.

As you walk along the north side of the square you will see below you what little remains of the medieval fortifications and the lovely harbour. Just before the corner you pass the theatre, the Teatro Borne. Turn left when you reach the Torre-Saura Palace (or after you have finished inspecting it) and leave the square by Carrer de Sa Muradeta, which first turns right and then left to bring you to the top of a wide flight of steps that take you down to the harbour. At the bottom turn left and walk along the quayside beneath the great walls, and maybe stop at one of the cafés for refreshment. Then continue alongside the harbour and turn left at the end to follow Carrer Marina up behind the city hall. Where the street turns left you will see a flight of steps ahead. Go up these steps, and cross Camí de Sant Nicolau to the park opposite, the Plaça de S'Esplanada. This is where the Torres bus stops are situated, and tourists coming from the beaches (and motorists) are recommended to begin the walk here.

[2] Walk away from the bus stops the length of the tree-filled park, leaving the Born Square and its obelisk behind you. This is where the first section of the walls once stood.

At the end of the park you come to the beginning of the avenues that continue the line of the former walls. The first one is Avinguda del Capità Negrete, and here you turn left. Captain Negrete had the misfortune to be the senior army officer in Ciutadella on the day the Turks sailed into the harbour. He had under him forty soldiers whom he had brought from Castille to repair the town's defences. Local territorials brought the number of armed men up to about 620. Pass two streets, Carrer Joan Benejam i Vives, and Carrer Nou de Juliol, and turn left along the third, Carrer Purissima. This leads back to the Born and, on the corner with the Plaça d'es Born, is the church of St Francis (Sant Francesc). Architecturally it is a mixture of 14th-century Gothic that survived the destruction and restoration baroque. When James II of Mallorca succeeded Alfonso in 1291 (he was only 23 when he died) he appointed a Royal Commission to organise Menorcan affairs which met in this church.

Just before the end of Carrer Purissima, opposite the church, turn right along Carrer de Sant Francesc. At the end, turn left along Carrer de Sant Jeroni. This street is bordered on the right by one of the older mansions, that of the Sintas family. At the junction with Carrer dels Dolors turn right and pass (on the left) the Plazuela del Rosario. Turn left along the next street, Carrer Roser: on the right is a visual treat, the gorgeous little church of Our Lady of the Rosary, from which the street gets its name. (This church too was vandalised during the Civil War.) It was begun at the end of the 17th century by the Dominican friars. When the British came in 1708 they requisitioned it and held Church of England services there for the benefit of the British soldiers. The extravagant baroque decoration of the main doorway is, like the Chapel of the Immaculate Conception in the church of St Francis in Mahón, decidedly churrigueresque. It now hosts exhibitions.

As you make your way to the end of Carrer Roser, you will see the Gothic south door of St Mary's Cathedral facing you. On reaching the Plaça de Pio XII once more, cross to the far left-hand corner where, opposite the west entrance to the cathedral, is the home of the Olives family. This mansion was built early in the 17th century. It contains much fine furniture, some made in the 18th century by Menorcan craftsmen from English pattern books, and some French from the time of the brief French occupation of the island (1756-63). Also French is the frieze featuring birds, animals and fishes which runs round the top of the walls in the three large state rooms.

Turn right and continue along Carrer del Ca'l Bisbe, passing on your right the Bishop's Palace. Christianity arrived early in Menorca, and there was a bishopric here until 484, when the last bishop, Makarius, sailed for North Africa to defend his faith before the heretical Vandal king, Hunnericus, never to be heard of again. Not until 1795 did the Vatican restore its bishop to Menorca and, as had been the case in the past, he chose Ciutadella to be his see. Previously his palace had been an Augustinian convent.

Facing the end of the street is yet another fine house, the Squella mansion, home of the Marqués de Menas Albas. It was here that the American Admiral David Farragut slept when he visited Ciutadella in December 1867. The bedroom and bed he used are still preserved. Farragut may well be unknown to English readers, but to Americans he is as important as Nelson. It was during the American Civil War that he made a name for himself, by sinking eleven Confederate warships and capturing New Orleans. He was put in command of all the naval forces and created First Admiral of the US Navy in 1866. The admiral's father was born in Ciutadella and had emigrated to the States when he was seventeen. During a goodwill visit of the American fleet to Mahón harbour, Admiral Farragut took the opportunity to visit his father's birthplace. Ciutadella took him to its heart. He was fêted and made an honorary citizen. There is a bust of him by the harbour mouth, near the Esmeralda Hotel.

Turn right at the junction, into Carrer Sant Sebastià. Pass Carrer de ses Andrones on the left, and turn along the next street on the left, Carrer Sant Cristòfol. Then take the second street on the right, Carrer Climent, go under the arch and carry on in the same direction along Carrer del Dormidor de les Monges (Padre Federico Pareja).

On the left is the convent of St Clare, founded through the generosity of Alfonso the Liberal in 1287. Destroyed by the Turks, the convent was rebuilt in the 17th century. To finance this the order imitated a practice initiated by Fr Miguel Subirats, the Prior of the Augustinians, to restore his convent (now the Bishop's Palace). They secured from the King of Spain the privilege of offering deeds of nobility to members of wealthy families in return for contributions. Many of the noble families whose houses you see on the walk acquired their titles in this way. The convent was restored once more in 1945. In 1987, on the 700th anniversary of its foundation, a plaque was put up recording its history.

Turn left along Carrer de María Auxiliadora, passing the sanctuary of the Salesian Fathers and, at the end, turn left along Avinguda de Francesc de Borja Moll and follow the line of the last section of wall to the Plaça de Sa Font or 'Fountain Square' (a drinking fountain, that is). Here you can see the only section of wall still remaining other than by the harbour.

Walk across the square and go along Carrer de Sa Muradeta to the left of the tower that is home to the municipal museum. The ground falls away steeply on your right, giving a view of small terraced gardens on both slopes of the valley. The wide sandy expanse below is Es Pla de Sant Joan (St John the Baptist). Notice how the steps lead down through all the gardens to terraces or platforms beside the wall which look out over Es Pla. That is where Menorca's most prestigious festival takes place annually on June 24th, the feast of St John the Baptist. The ceremony goes back to the Middle Ages. It begins with a cavalcade of over a hundred richly caparisoned horses, their riders (*caixers*) in traditional costume. The cavalcade is led by a man bearing the flag of the Knights of St John of Malta. There follow displays of horsemanship, with prancing steeds, and young men doing their best to make them unseat their riders, all to the accompaniment of pipes and tambourines and general merriment. Then these terraces will be thronged with onlookers getting the best — and safest — view of the proceedings.

Towards the end of Carrer de Sa Muradeta, immediately before the steps going down to the port, turn left into Carrer de Pere Capllonch. Ignore Carrer des Forn on the right, and turn left again into Carrer Sant Rafel. Now is the time to let your imagination have free rein. If ever there were streets which allowed you to pass back through time, they are these alleyways. But do remember that though the layout of the streets may be medieval, or even Moorish, the houses themselves cannot predate 1558. All had to be rebuilt after the Turkish destruction.

Pass on the right the junction with Carrer Sant Sebastià, and follow the street as it turns first right, and then left, into Carrer Sant Miquel. On the right you will pass the church of San Miguel. At the end of the street turn right into Carrer St Jaume and, almost at once, go left at the junction with Carrer Sant Bartomeu. Enter Carrer de Ses

Roques and at the following junction turn right through 130 degrees. After 25m/yds turn left once more into Carrer de Santa Helena.

Turn right at the T-junction along Portal de Sa Font (Carrer Fuente). Very soon you pass the convent of Santa Clara again, on your left. In the 18th century the convent was the scene of a scandal straight from the pages of a 'Mills and Boon'. The saintly sisters ran a school for young ladies. With the ingenuity of young ladies the world over, three of the pupils managed both to make the acquaintance of, and to fall in love with, a trio of young English army officers. With determined recklessness, the girls fled the convent and hid with the lieutenants, rejecting all attempts to persuade them to return. The Roman Catholic church was up in arms. The girls must be returned to the convent. The governor, General Blakeney, showing a remarkable broadness of mind, refused to force them back against their will. All were duly wed and, I suppose, lived happily ever after.

Keep going in the same direction and enter Carrer Santa Clara. On your right is one of the oldest and most prestigious of the stately homes of Ciutadella. No 29 is the palace of the Barons of Lluriach, the oldest of the Menorcan titles. Its facade shows that stern rejection of ostentation that characterises so many Spanish buildings. It is an impressive building nonetheless.

At the end of Carrer Santa Clara cross over Ses Voltes (Carrer J M Quadrado) and go along Carrer d'es Seminari. There are three fine buildings here, all on your left. The first is the church of Santo Cristo, a tiny baroque gem, built in 1667 and restored just three hundred years later. Outside it has classical columns and capitals and an octagonal stone dome surmounted by a stone lantern. Within, unbelievably, there is a tiny gallery. Lower down the street is a bank which is housed in one of the town's former mansions — a mansion with a story. The British first came to Menorca because of their involvement in the War of the Spanish Succession. King Carlos II of Spain had died childless, and there were two young claimants to the throne, descended from his sisters. One was French, Prince Philip of Anjou, the other Austrian, the Archduke Charles. Inevitably Britain was determined that it could not be the Frenchman. In the war that ensued, the Royal Navy was hampered by having to return to England every winter, and General James Stanhope saw the value to Britain in having the use of Mahón harbour.

He gained the support of the pro-Austrian party on Menorca, whose leader was Juán Miguel Saura y Morell. In revenge the pro-French party burned his home to the ground. After Stanhope had conquered the island, he had a splendid new house built in Ciutadella for Saura — the one occupied today by the bank. The third curiosity is yet another church towards the end of the street, now a concert hall. Next door is the diocesan museum.

Turn right at the end of Carrer d'es Seminari into Carrer Santissim. Halfway along pass a street on the left, which you will eventually follow. But before doing so, walk to the end of the street and look at the building on your left. Now partly an antique shop, it is the palace of the Saura family and was built towards the end of the 17th century. It is finely proportioned, with beautiful neo-classical decorations round the full-length windows on the first floor. Inside is a broad staircase made in 1718, and the reception rooms are lit by magnificent chandeliers made in La Granja, near Madrid. On the other side of Carrer Santissim is the Martorell Palace, home of the Marqués de Albranca. Like the Lluriach Palace, its façade is reserved in decoration, exhibiting again that Spanish architectural puritanism.

Return now to the street you passed earlier, and turn along Carrer del Portal d'Artruix. Shortly, take the first turning on the left, Carrer Castell Rupit. After some 80m/yds you reach the Plaça de la Libertat, built in 1868 and today home to Ciutadella's market.

At the end of Carrer Castell Rupit turn right along Carrer Sant Onofre, and soon you will come to the Avinguda Jaume I El Conqueridor. 'Conqueror' is the title bestowed on King James I of Aragon for the reconquest of Catalonia and Mallorca. He began the reconquest of Menorca which his grandson Alfonso completed. He did not actually invade the smaller island, but terrified its Moorish rulers into becoming his vassals.

Turn left along Conqueridor and bear left into Avinguda de la Constitució for some 200m/yds. You have now arrived back at the Plaça d'Alfons III where the walk began. Those who started at [2] should now turn back to [1] on page 112 and continue the walk from there. The Mahón bus will be found by turning right at the traffic lights and walking along the Camí de Maó as far as the first street on the right, which is Carrer Barcelona, where the TMSA depot is. Carry on along the Avinguda de la Constitució for the Cala Morell mini-bus stop.

**See town plan on pages 114-115 and map on pages 126-127**
**Distance:** each walk 4km/2.5mi; 1h           **Grade:** easy
**Equipment:** comfortable shoes of any sort, sunhat, raingear, suncream
**How to get there and return:** as Walk 20, page 112; begin at the Born Square (Plaça d'es Born), shown below.

These two short walks — especially suitable for an evening *paseo* before the late dinner hour — are pleasant alternatives to strolling round the Old City and give you a taste of rural Menorca.

### Walk 21-1
**Start out** by walking away from the Born Square across the tree-bedecked Plaça de S'Esplanada, and turn left at the far side along Avinguda del Capità Negrete. The avenue bends to the left and changes its name to Conqueridor (in honour of James I the Conqueror). After 100m/yds you come to the little Plaça d'Artruix on the left. (It was formerly called Plaza de Cabrisas y Caymaris, in honour of a Ciutadellan who emigrated to Cuba, made his fortune, and returned to Menorca to establish its shoemaking industry.)

Cross the avenue and follow Carrer de Mossèn Josep Salord i Farnès opposite. Cross over Carrer de Francesc Fivaller, and soon you will come to the Plaça de Jaume II. Keep to the right of the square, and leave it in the

*The Plaça d'es Born was the creation of the early 19th century. A hundred years of British rule had brought a previously unknown prosperity to the island, and the recently-renewed link with Spain had aroused considerable national pride. This square was its outward expression, and the aristocracy rebuilt their palaces to adorn it.*

opposite right-hand corner by Camí de Sant Joan de Missa. Ignore the street on the right and go over a bridge. Immediately beyond the bridge turn left and then right, and follow the road round to the left at the top. Only a few houses and farms border this quiet cul-de-sac.

After 1km/0.6mi the road bends sharply left and, in a few metres, just as sharply to the right, beneath power lines (**22min**). Do not follow the road to the right, but take the walled-in track straight ahead. In 350m/yds ignore a similar track to the right, and head in the direction of Ciutadella along this ancient cart-road. Ignore a second turning on the right and look out for a curious gateway on the left. Pass a turning on the left, and one more on the right before reaching Ciutadella. When you pass the cemetery (on the right; **45min**), cross over the road ahead and go along Carrer de la Creu opposite. Pass the end of Carrer Cautivos de Constantinoble on the right, and cross over Carrer Vila Juaneda, to enter Carrer Barcelona. Turn left at the end and follow the Camí de Maó to the Plaça d'Alfons III. Enter the old city by the facing street, Carrer de Maó, and walk straight back to Born Square (**1h**).

## Walk 21-2
**Start out** by crossing Born Square. Pass the obelisk, and leave by Carrer de Sa Muradeta in the corner nearest the harbour. Walk along that street past the steps leading down to the port and continue to the end, looking down on the sandy Plá de Sant Joan. When you reach the old tower, continue along Avinguda de Francesc de Borja Moll opposite. Instead of turning right at the end along the Avinguda de la Constitució, cross over and keep going in the same direction along Carrer Alfons XIII. Keep to the left at the end and continue in the same direction along Carrer de Màrius Verdaguer, named in honour of Menorca's foremost man of letters.

Turn left after 100m/yds and you are suddenly in farming country (**12min**). From here follow the track on the right (Camí de ses Capelletes). After 600m/0.35mi you come to a junction: take either of the tracks forking to the left or the right ahead (rather than the paths going off at right angles), and follow them into increasingly remote and pleasant countryside. As farm after farm peels off, so the tracks become narrower and narrower until, reaching the last farm of all, they stop altogether (each route about **30min**). Now you must retrace your steps (**1h**), but I think you will agree that it has been worthwhile walking out.

## 22 THE NAVETA D'ES TUDONS

**See also town plan pages 114-115**

**Distance:** 13km/8mi; 3h

**Grade:** moderat

**Equipment:** comfortable footwear, sunhat, raingear, suncream, picnic, plenty of water, torch

**How to get there and return:** 🚌 to/from Ciutadella. Or 🚗 to/from the Naveta d'es Tudons. Drive along the C721 to the *naveta* where there is excellent parking, and begin the walk at that point, following it into Ciutadella and back to the *naveta*.

**Short walk:** Naveta d'es Tudons — Ciutadella (5km/3mi; 1h20min; easy; grade, equipment as above). Access/return: 🚌 to/from the TMSA depot in Carrer Barcelona in Ciutadella. You buy your ticket in the office, not on the bus, so be sure you tell the driver that you want to get off at the Naveta d'es Tudons. You will reach it about five minutes after leaving the depot. Begin at the *naveta* (plainly visible from the road) and follow the main walk from the 1h46min-point back to Ciutadella.

**P**erhaps the most celebrated cyclopean building on Menorca is the large burial chamber visible on the left, four kilometres short of Ciutadella as you approach from Ferreries. Various claims have been made for it, including that it is the oldest roofed building in Spain, or indeed Europe. It is certainly a very interesting edifice, and the best of the *navetas*, in that it contains two storeys and has been extensively restored. This walk not only visits the *naveta*, but takes you through some very pleasant and quiet countryside in the vicinity of Ciutadella.

Referring to the plan on pages 114-115, **begin the walk** at the TMSA bus terminus in Carrer Barcelona off the Camí de Maó in Ciutadella. (If you intend coming by bus from the Mahón direction along the C721 and are only going to do the short walk, you can save time and money by asking to be put down at the Naveta d'es Tudons. It would be as well to remind the driver of this shortly after leaving Ferreries.) Walk away from the Camí de Maó along Carrer Barcelona, and cross over Carrer Vila Juaneda. Fork left, and continue along Carrer de la Creu, passing a number of automobile workshops. Follow the street as it turns left, and pass the junction with Carrer Cautivos de Constantinoble (which commemorates the 3495 inhabitants of Ciutadella who in the year 1558 were carried off by the Turks to Constantinople, to be sold as slaves).

Carry on towards the open country which you can now see ahead, crossing over Carrer Glosador Vivó. At the crossroads, head for the white wall opposite. Behind the pine trees on your left is the municipal cemetery. When you reach the white wall, turn right and follow the sandy cart-track as it bends to the left. Ignore the path on the left that you reach almost at once. Ahead you can see the Ciutadella electricity substation. The advantage of this is that you can readily check where you are as you pass beneath the power lines which radiate out from it. Soon you pass a surprisingly elaborate gateway on your right (**10min**). As the track winds along, a couple of paths go off to the left; ignore them. Keep to the main cart-track (it is still used by horse-drawn carts) until eventually you come out on to a tarmac road at a bend (**30min**).

Turn left, walk past the pylon and under the power lines. You will follow this country road for roughly 3km/2mi. There is very little traffic on it however, since (despite its length) it is a cul-de-sac and only provides access to one or two farms. Twice more you will pass under power lines, at intervals of about 1.5km/1mi. At first the lane passes through flat, rather uninteresting country, but soon it becomes more undulating, with increasingly attractive scenery and a healthy chorus of birdsong. You will find the fields marked with two different warning notices. There is the ubiquitous *Coto Privado de Caza,* which replaces the English favourite: 'Trespassers Will Be Prosecuted'. It means 'Private Shooting'. On the mainland the cautionary phrase is often abbreviated to just one word: *Coto.* Here an alternative is often found, a rectangle divided diagonally into black and white triangles.

After two miles you walk between two farms — Binipati Nou and Binipati Pons. There is a bend in the road, and the tarmac ends with a turning circle (**1h**). Continue along the track and shortly come to a gate. After the gate, follow the track towards the visually pleasing farmhouse of Sa Trinitá (La Trinidad). Turn left in front of the house (**1h15min**) and follow the track as it bends to the right and passes to the left of the farmhouse. Go through another gateway and continue beside the farm. Cross a cattle grid and in five minutes enter an area of woodland, where the song of the birds will attain even more decibels. Go through two more gates before emerging from the wood to cross what might be described as open parkland. This track continues through lovely country for 1.5km/1mi from Sa Trinitá. Where it ends, climb over a padlocked gate, to a narrow asphalt road (**1h30min**).

Turn left here. Very soon you will see on your left one of those massive, solid old farmhouses built with one apprehensive eye on the North African corsairs who were the curse of Menorcan history, and the other on the equally troublesome bandits (some of whom, in 1636,

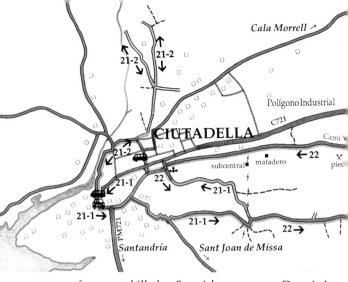

went so far as to kill the Spanish governor, Don Juán Valenciano de Mendiolaza!) The farm is Es Tudons. Opposite the entrance, go over a cattle grid on the right of the road and through a gate. Walk forward along the path and, in 100m/yds, you will see the *naveta* of Es Tudons on your left (**1h46min**; photograph page 128). *(Those of you who came by car, as well as those doing the Short walk, begin here.)*

When you leave the *naveta*, turn right and follow the path for a 100m/yds, until you reach the field gate and cattle grid and emerge on the tarmac road opposite the

---

### THE NAVETA D'ES TUDONS

In the 1950s the *naveta* was in a lamentable condition and in danger of total destruction. It was overgrown with bushes, and one end was broken open. Its present splendid state is due to the enthusiasm of two people. One was Luís Pericot García, Professor of Archaeology at the University of Barcelona, who conceived and masterminded the restoration. The other was María Luisa Serra Belabre, then Director of Mahón Museum, to whom the work was entrusted. She was aided by an architect named Victor Tolor. A grant from the March Foundation in 1958 made the work possible, and the excavation of the site and restoration of the *naveta* was undertaken in 1959/60. Bushes were removed, fallen stones restored to their proper places, and additional stones obtained from the same quarry whence the original ones had come. During the excavations María Serra found hundreds of human bones, from at least a hundred bodies, lying on a bed of pebbles. Bronze bracelets still encircled some of the arm bones. Other bronze items and simple jewellery that had been buried with the corpses were also found. The entrance is narrow and low, but not difficult, and inside there is a vestibule and two chambers, one above the other, both of which were used for burials.

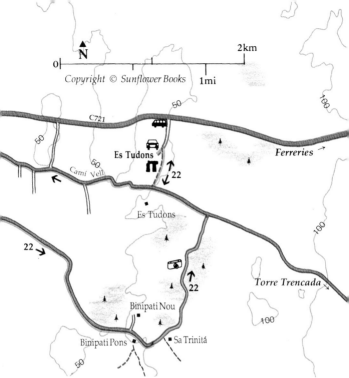

farmhouse of Es Tudons. Turn right, and walk back to Ciutadella along this road, a distance of 4km/2.5mi. As you start off, notice the section of old road on your right. At this point a detour was made, perhaps when the ruts became too deep for comfort and, fortunately, the tarmac followed the line of the detour. For this is no simple country lane. It is the Camí Vell — the 'Old Road', built by the Romans before the birth of Christ and used by travellers leaving Ciutadella for the south for over seventeen centuries — until Sir Richard Kane built his new road across the island in the 18th century. Keep on this road, as it winds and twists in a most un-Roman way, and ignore any side turnings to right or left.

What can you look out for in the next hour? You will be aware by now of the red kites which are almost always circling above you, wherever you are walking in Menorca; huge birds, and unmistakable, with deeply forked tails and white patches beneath their wings. If you are in luck, you may see a rarer species along this road. Nearly the size of a kite, its tail is wedge-shaped, not forked. Black when

*Red kite*

*The Naveta d'es Tudons*

seen from beneath, when it swoops in the valley below you there is a broad band of white across the top of its wings. That bird is the booted eagle. It was here that I once saw one.

As you climb the hill on the far side of the valley, look out for the circular stone threshing floors near the farms on your right (**2h15min**). Weighted sledges would be dragged round by oxen or donkeys (I once saw one being dragged by tractor on the mainland) over the cut corn, separating the wheat grains from the chaff as they did so. Getting closer to Ciutadella, there are the stone quarries ('*piedra*' on the map) to see. If it is a work day you will see workmen cutting the stones out of the rock. A characteristic of this limestone is that it is quite soft and easy to cut, until it is exposed to the air, when it becomes quite the opposite — very hard indeed.

Over to your right, close to the main road, there is a *talayot*, quite overgrown with bushes. Then Ciutadella comes into sight, the cathedral prominent. Raise your eyes and beyond the city you will see the distant fortified farmhouse of Torre del Ram. Some may find the next building on the left, discreetly hidden behind trees, more macabre. It is the *matadero*, the abattoir. Next you pass the substation, and shortly you arrive back in town. Turn right at the junction, along Carrer Sant Antoni M Claret and, at the traffic lights, turn left along the Camí de Maó. In four minutes you will be back at Carrer Barcelona and the TMSA bus depot (**3h**). Walkers who left their car at the *naveta* should now turn to the start of the walk and follow the notes from there, to return to the site by a different route.

## 23 CURNIOLA AND THE CAVES OF CALA MORELL

**Distance:** 8.3km/5.1mi; 2h45min     **See also drawings pages 17, 63**

**Grade:** moderate

**Equipment:** walking boots (preferably, otherwise comfortable shoes or trainers), sunhat, raingear, suncream, picnic, plenty of water, swimwear, towel, binoculars

**How to get there and return:** mini-🚐 or 🚌 to/from Cala Morell. The mini-🚐 service is infrequent, so be prepared to make a day of it. The bus stop is in the Avinguda de la Constitució in Ciutadella, just north of the Plaça d'Alfons III and the junction with the Mahón road. By 🚌, follow the central avenues in Ciutadella northwards, turning right to follow signs for Cala Morell. Motorists coming from Ferreries can avoid Ciutadella centre by turning right by the Leo shoe factory and driving across the industrial estate. Turn right at the end along the Camí de la Vall. On reaching Cala Morell, park in the car park on the right.

**Shorter walk:** To shorten the walk by 30 minutes, you can ask the mini-🚐 driver to put you off at the Bini Atrám junction, where the bus turns left to head north to Cala Morell (point to it on your map). Start the walk at the 30min-point and continue to the end, returning by bus as above.

A very enjoyable walk, this route circles the impressive farmhouse of Curniola, partly through agricultural land and partly through pine woods, and then goes on to explore one of the most important Bronze Age cave settlements in Europe. As a bonus you can while away the time waiting for your return bus by swimming in the clearest water surrounding Menorca.

**Begin the walk** by heading back towards Ciutadella along the road by which you have come. In **9min** you pass the entrance to Curniola and have your first glimpse of the imposing villa which will be your constant companion for the remainder of the walk. In **10min** you are opposite another farmhouse — Bini Atrám, while ahead and to the right you can see in the distance one of the most famous farmhouses on the island, the massively defended Torre d'en Quart (see page 63). You may have noticed it on your way from Ciutadella. If not, look at it on the way back. Its tower is enormous. These sturdy dwellings with their defensive towers are a feature of the island. Found also on the mainland in Catalonia, they remind us that Menorca's *calas* attracted quite a different kind of foreign visitor in earlier times — pirates!

Some **30min** after leaving Cala Morell you come to a T-junction. *(The Shorter walk starts here.)* If you turn left you will discover a walled-in track between the two tarmac roads. Turn along this cart-track, and in five minutes pass on your right the entrance to Son Seu farm.

Go through the gate of Bini Atrám. The track twists across fields to an iron gate. Continue to the right of the

129

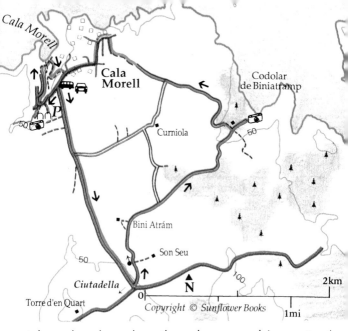

Cala Morell

**Cala Morell**

Codolar de Biniatramp

Curniola

Bini Atrám

Son Seu

*Ciutadella*

Torre d'en Quart

P

50

50

60

50

100

2km

**N**

0

1mi

*Copyright © Sunflower Books*

telegraph pole and on through a second iron gate. A minute later, ignore the track on the left which goes to Curniola (**45min**), and keep straight on. In four minutes go through another iron gate and across a field, and in five minutes enter a pine wood. If you look to your left at this point (and if your luck is in) you may see Menorca's most colourful bird — the bee-eater. After yet another iron gate you pass a cottage on the left, but keep to the right here, going uphill and still in woodland. Besides the bee-eater, keep your eye open for another example of local fauna that I have seen in this wood — the tortoise. About 13 minutes beyond the last gate you will come upon a small building with a garden full of children's playthings (**1h10min**). If it is a Sunday or bank holiday it will be full of children playing on them too. Here you will eventually turn left but, before doing so, walk to the right of the house and continue along the track for a couple of hundred metres/yards, until you reach the sea at the Codolar de Biniatramp.

Then return to the children's playground, turn right and walk beside the boundary wall as far as a facing wall. If you look closely, you will see that what was formerly a gap has been walled in, so that now you must climb over to get into the field. Cross the field in the same northwesterly direction, past a worked-out sand quarry and on towards woodland. At the far side of the field the track swings left, enters the pine wood and doubles back to the right, skirting the wood. There are plenty of open shady places to rest, or picnic. Some 10 minutes after climbing the wall, the track turns left away from the wood and you reach an iron gate. Beyond the gate the track continues along the edge of a field with shrubs to the right, once more northwestwards, shortly keeping to the right of a wall.

In nine minutes ignore a track on the left; continue to walk beside the wall and, in 20m/yds, go through an iron gate and over a cattle grid. Carry on along the track and climb over a wall. Soon you reach the corner of the wall. Ahead is another former sand quarry. Walk to the right of the workings, heading for the far right-hand corner of the field. Here you climb a low wall into a small field of heather. Follow a path to the nearest concrete post ahead. You will discover that it houses a street lamp. Walk to the end of the street (Lleo Menor) and turn left into Auriga. Pass the end of Cassiopea and bear left at the roundabout into Via Lactia, which you follow to the right and downhill to the bus stop at Cala Morell (**2h15min**). Keep straight ahead, ignoring the road to Ciutadella on your left, and follow the lane downhill. It is not long before you see on your left the first pair of caves for which Cala Morell is famous. After exploring these, carry on down the hill, to where a bridge crosses over the *barranco*. The main troglodytic village is situated just before this bridge. Footpaths fork to each side of the hill on your left, and both lead to caves. Most of them are on the left, where they are to be found in the cliffs on both sides of a small valley (Picnic 4).

---

### THE CAVES

There are many things to look out for, but their sophistication is probably what impresses most. There are paths chipped out of the rock to provide access to them; often windows light them. Usually a central pillar was left to give support to the roof. Frequently niches and troughs have been carved out, and in several there is a raised area where probably the family slept. As you move up the valley you will come across even more sophisticated features. There is a channel carved out of the cliff face that directs rainwater down into a trough cut out of the cliff, which overflows into an irrigation channel. Another larger channel collects rainwater on the other side of the valley and conveys it to where it was required for irrigation. One cave has an elaborate façade carved in high relief to give it the appearance of an Egyptian dwelling. Also of interest are the oval cavities cut into the cliff face (see drawing page 17). Similar cavities are found all over the island. Local people called them 'capades de Moro' and attributed them to a Moorish passion for head banging! Their purpose can only be guessed at, and it is assumed that it was funerary, perhaps for holding urns containing bones or ashes, or maybe offerings were placed in them. Near the end of the little valley there is a bridge. Go beyond it to the cave on the right. It has two outstanding features — raised sleeping quarters and a magnificently carved chimney. However, by the year 1000BC people had moved out of even these fine caves into the 'more fashionable' talayotic settlements, and for the next thousand years they were used for burials.

When you have seen this central part of the village, return to the road and go up the path to the right of the hill. You will soon see two caves some distance away, but as you walk towards them you will discover what seem to be tiny paths cut out from the rock and, when you reach the caves, there is quite an elaborate road carved to the left of them. These caves connect, and the one on the left is surrounded with little stone troughs.

When you have done with the caves, you may wish to sample Cala Morell's other attraction, its swimming. Return to the road and turn left. At the next junction turn right and follow the road down to the beach (a gate part way down prohibits cars). As well as the beach, there is a system of rock paths and sunbathing terraces. Steps lead up to restaurants, bars, and the *urbanización*. The last is rather chic. The street lamps are concealed in what look like concrete gnomes watching your progress through the village. If they all work, it could look very romantic after dark. Finally return to the bus stop or your car (**2h45min**). To avoid Ciutadella, motorists from the south can drive across the industrial estate again, but a one way system demands a slightly different route. Follow the signs for 'Maó'.

*Cala Morell, seen from one of the hillside caves*

# BUS TIMETABLES

Most buses are operated by Transportes Menorca SA (TMSA). The main bus stations are in Mahón (J M Quadrado 7; telephone 36.03.61) and Ciutadella (Barcelona 8; telephone 38.03.93). Numbers following the place names below refer to **timetable** numbers. *Timetables are subject to change without notice; be sure to obtain up-to-date timetables from the stations or the tourist office. Journey times are approximate.*

| | | |
|---|---|---|
| Alaior 1, 9 | Cala'n Porter 7 | Punta Prima 4 |
| Alcaufar 5 | Ciutadella 1, 13-16 | S'Algar 5 |
| Arenal d'en Castell 11 | Club San Jaime 9 | Santandría 14 |
| Binibeca 6 | Es Castell 2 | Sant Lluís 3 |
| Cala Blanca 14 | Es Grau 8 | Sant Tomàs 10, |
| Cala Morell 16 | Es Mercadal 1 | 13 |
| Cala Santa Galdana 12, | Ferreries 1, 17 | Son Bou 9 |
| 17 | Fornells 11 | Son Parc 11 |
| Cala'n Bosch 15 | Mahón/Maó 1-12 | Son Xoriguer 15 |

## SERVICES TO AND FROM MAHON

**1 Mahón—Alaior—Es Mercadal—Ferreries—Ciutadella** *daily, from J M Quadrado 7 in Mahón and Carrer Barcelona 8 in Ciutadella. Journey times: Alaior 15min, Es Mercadal 30min, Ferreries 45min, Ciutadella 1h15min*
Departs Mahón 08.00, 10.00, 11.30, 13.00, 16.30, 19.00
Departs Ciutadella 08.00, 10.00, 11.30, 14.30, 16.30, 19.00

**2 Mahón—Es Castell** *daily, from J M Quadrado 7. Journey time 10min*
Departs Mahón 07.20*, 07.45*, 08.15*, 08.45*; then half-hourly from 09.15 to 10.45; from 11.45 to 16.45; and from 17.45 to 20.45
Departs Es Castell 07.30*, 08.00*, 08.30*, 09.00*; then half-hourly from 09.30 to 11.00; from 12.00 to 17.00; and from 18.00 to 21.00

**3 Mahón—Sant Lluís** *daily, from J M Quadrado 7. Journey time 10min*
Departs Mahón 08.10*, 08.30; then hourly from 09.30 to 13.30; from 15.30 to 19.30; a last bus departs 20.15
Departs Sant Lluís 07.30*, 08.20; then hourly from 09.10 to 13.10; from 15.10 to 19.10; a last bus departs 20.00

**4 Mahón—Punta Prima** *daily, from J M Quadrado 7. Journey time 25min*
Departs Mahón 08.30*; hourly from 09.30 to 13.30; and finally at 16.30, 18.30 and 19.30
Departs Punta Prima (in front of Hotel Xaloc) 09.00*; hourly from 10.00 to 14.00; and finally at 17.00, 19.00 and 20.00

**5 Mahón—Alcaufar—S'Algar** *daily, from J M Quadrado 7. Journey times: Alcaufar 15mi, S'Algar 30min*
Departs Mahón 08.30, 09.30, 12.30, 13.30, 15.30, 18.30
Departs Alcaufar 08.45, 09.45, 12.45, 13.45, 15.45, 18.45
Departs S'Algar 09.00, 10.00, 13.00, 14.00, 16.00, 19.00

**6 Mahón—Binibeca** *daily, from J M Quadrado 7. Journey time 25min*
Departs Mahón †10.30, 14.20, 17.30; Departs Binibeca 11.00, 14.45, 18.00

**7 Mahón—Sant Climent—Son Vitamina—Cala'n Porter** *daily (except Sun/holidays), from Plaça de S'Esplanada . Journey times: Sant Climent 10min, Son Vitamina 15min, Cala'n Porter 25min*
Departs Mahón 09.30, 10.30, 11.45, 13.15, 16.00, 18.00, 19.30
Departs Cala'n Porter 10.00, 11.00, 12.15, 13.45, 16.30, 18.30, 20.00

*except Sun/holidays; ■ only on Sun/holidays; † except Sat/Sun/holidays

133

**8 Mahón—Es Grau** *daily, from Plaça de S'Esplanada (July-Sept only).*
*Journey time 25min*
Departs Mahón 10.00, 11.00■, 12.00*, 13.00■, 17.00
Departs Es Grau 10.30, 11.30■, 12.30*, 13.30■, 17.30

**9 Mahón—Alaior—Son Bou** *daily (except Sun/holidays), from Plaça de S'Esplanada. Journey times: Alaior 15min, Son Bou 25min, Club San Jaime 30min ·*
Departs Mahón 08.50, 10.00, 13.00, 14.00, 19.00
Departs Son Bou 09.30, 10.30, 13.30, 16.00, 19.30
Also **Mahón—Club San Jaime**: depart 10.00, 14.00, 19.00; departs Club San Jaime: 10.30, 16.00, 19.30

**10 Mahón—Sant Tomàs** *daily (except Sun/holidays), from Plaça de S'Esplanada. Journey time 45min*
Departs Mahón 12.45; Departs Santo Tomàs 09.15

**11 Mahón—Arenal d'en Castell—Son Parc—Fornells** *daily, from the corner of the Plaça de S'Esplanada and Carrer Vassalo (private bus company, not TMSA). Journey times: Arenal 30min, Son Parc 55min, Fornells 1h10min*
Departs Mahón 11.00, 13.00*, 19.00
Departs Fornells 08.30■, 09.00*, 15.45*, 17.00■
Departs Son Parc 15min later and Arenal 40min later

**12 Mahón—Cala Santa Galdana** *daily (except Sun/holidays) from the Plaça de S'Esplanada. Journey time 1h*
Departs Mahón 09.00, 12.15
Departs Cala Santa Galdana 08.00, 10.00

## SERVICES TO AND FROM CIUTADELLA: see also (1) above

**13 Ciutadella—Sant Tomàs** *not daily (TMSA, Barcelona 8). Journey time 1h*
Departs Ciutadela 19.00†; Departs Santo Tomàs 15.00†

**14 Ciutadella—Santandría—Cala Blanca** *daily**. Journey times: Santandría 10min, Cala Blanca 15min*
Departs Ciutadella 09.00, 10.10, 11.20, 12.10*, 13.20, 14.30*, 16.10, 17.10*, 18.10, 19.10, 20.10*, 21.10, 22.10; Returns 10 minutes later from Santandría, 15 minutes later from Cala Blanca

**15 Ciutadella—Cala'n Bosch—Son Xoriguer** *daily**. Journey times: Cala'n Bosch 15min, Son Xoriguer 20min*
Departs Ciutadella 08.15*, 09.00, 10.00, 11.00, 11.45*, 12.30, 13.15, 14.00*, 15.00*, 16.00, 17.00, 18.00, 19.00, 20.20, 21.25, 22.30; Returns 20 minutes later

**16 Ciutadella—Cala Morell** *daily mini-bus service, departing from the Avda de la Constitució near Carrer Federico Pareja. Journey time 15min*
Departs Ciutadella 08.30, 13.00, 18.30; Returns 15 minutes later

## SERVICES TO AND FROM FERRERIAS (run by TMSA)

**17 Ferreries—Cala Santa Galdana** *daily (except Sun/holidays). Journey time 15min*
Departs Ferreries 07.45, 09.45, 13.00, 13.30, 15.00, 16.45, 17.00, 18.30
Departs Cala Santa Galdana 08.00, 10.00, 13.15, 15.15, 16.30, 17.30, 18.45, 19.30

*except Sun/holidays; ■ only on Sun/holidays; † except Sat/Sun/holidays; **private service of the Torres bus company, with departures from the Plaça de S'Esplanada

ographical names comprise the only entries in this index; for other
ries, see Contents, page 3. A page number in **bold type** indicates a
otograph or drawing, a page number in *italics* a map; both may be
addition to a text reference on the same page. (*TM* refers to the large-
le walking map on the reverse of the fold-out touring map).

## STOP PRESS

**Walk 2:** The 'gap in a wall' not far before the **50min**-point has been filled in, but stones have been placed beside it as a stile for you to climb over. (User, 6/96)

**Walk 11:** The owner of Atalitx farm no longer wishes walkers to cross his land. At the **2h49min**-point, turn *right* and walk back towards the sea along the path you came out on. Return to Son Bou along the beach or the dunes. You can still visit the *barrancos* by following this short walk: Make your way to the Son Bou car park behind the beach and, if sure-footed, follow the path through the marsh to the Club San Jaime bus stop. (If you are not sure-footed, walk up the hill through Son Bou, turn left at the junction and follow the bottom road to the Club San Jaime bus stop.) Turn left and follow the road beside the marsh to the end, then turn right. Shortly turn left through the car park of the Aparthotel Las Marismas, and go through an iron gate at the end. Follow a track across the Barranco d'es Bec. Ignore a track on your right through a field, and carry on ahead as the track bends left, bringing you to Ses Canassies farm. In four minutes ignore a track on the right, go through a gate, and pass Son Benet farm. In six minutes, after another gate, turn left and cross the Torrente de Son Bute. Now you have to retrace your steps or you will come to Atalitx farm. Follow the directions in the book from the 3h20min-point. (The Author, 10/96)

**Walk 13:** *IMPORTANT; THIS WALK IS NO LONGER POSSIBLE.* Users report that one of the landowners through whose land this walk passes is no longer allowing walkers to cross it. (The Author, 10/96)